At Issue

Body Piercing and Tattoos

Other Books in the At Issue Series:

At Issue

Body Piercing
and Tattoos

Tamara Roleff, Book Editor

GREENHAVEN PRESS

An imprint of Thomson Gale, a part of The Thomson Corporation

Detroit • New York • San Francisco • New Haven, Conn. • Waterville, Maine • London

Christine Nasso, *Publisher*
Elizabeth Des Chenes, *Managing Editor*

© 2008 The Gale Group.

Star logo is a trademark and Gale and Greenhaven Press are registered trademarks used herein under license.

For more information, contact:
Greenhaven Press
27500 Drake Rd.
Farmington Hills, MI 48331-3535
Or you can visit our Internet site at http://www.gale.com

LIBRARY OF CONGRESS CATALOGING-IN-PUBLICATION DATA

Body piercing and tattoos / Tamara Roleff, book editor.
    p. cm. -- (At issue)
Includes bibliographical references and index.
ISBN-13: 978-0-7377-3111-8 (hardcover)
ISBN-13: 978-0-7377-3112-5 (pbk.)
1. Body piercing. 2. Tattooing. I. Roleff, Tamara L., 1959-
GN419.25B63 2008
391.6'5--dc22

2007033050

ISBN-10: 0-7377-3111-7 (hardcover)
ISBN-10: 0-7377-3112-5 (pbk.)

Printed in the United States of America
10 9 8 7 6 5 4 3 2 1

Contents

Introduction

In 1985 Henry Ferguson was in a motorcycle accident. He suffered cracked ribs and vertebrae, and severe internal injuries to his spleen, kidneys, and gastric artery. At the hospital, he thought the staff seemed more interested in having him remove the jewelry in his various body piercings than in trying to save his life. Several years later, he met a nurse who told him a story about a badly injured patient who was ignored by the emergency room staff. Because the patient was a biker and had multiple body piercings, they were sure that he was gay and a sadomasochist, and therefore sure to have AIDS. Ferguson realized that the patient the nurse was describing was himself following his accident. It was only through the intervention of a surgeon that Ferguson's life was saved.

Devotees of body piercings and tattoos may hate to admit it, but they are often negatively judged by the public because of their body modifications. Much of this has to do with the preconceptions that people have about the types of people who have tattoos and body piercings; in the past, only convicts, sailors, gang members, outlaw bikers, carnival workers, and gay men were pierced or tattooed. While perceptions have mellowed over the decades, most people still think the only acceptable piercings are a single piercing in each ear for women and none at all for men. As for tattoos, people are more willing to accept a single tattoo on a man than one on a woman.

Ear piercings fell out of favor around the 1920s when clip-on earrings became popular. Starting in the 1960s, women started piercing their ears again, and the practice spread to hippies, gays, and then punk rock fans. Gay men usually pierced just one ear, although whether they pierced the right ear or the left ear to indicate the wearer's sexual orientation varied by locale. But as pierced ears on women became more common, heterosexual men also started piercing their ears and women began getting multiple piercings in their ears.

In the twenty-first century, it is perfectly acceptable for women to have pierced ears, even with multiple piercings, while some employers still frown on men with piercings, even pierced ears. The more conservative employers, such as financial institutions, often require their male employees to remove their pierced earrings when they are at work. And while women in the U.S. military may wear a single gold or pearl stud earring in each ear while on duty, male service members are prohibited from having pierced ears and may face disciplinary action if they wear pierced earrings even while off duty. Many employers feel the same way as a recruiter for a construction engineering firm explained:

> There might be a double standard in our society, but male students with body art, especially body piercings such as eyebrow, nose, tongue and lip piercings give the impression of an individual that might not fit in or be willing to conform to a corporate image or environment.

Perhaps society's disapproval of men with pierced ears is due to the fact that earrings are considered a female attribute; men with earrings are not conforming to society's expectations of male gender roles, and so are judged negatively.

Tattoos, while increasingly more common on both men and women—especially on women—have not yet reached the level of respectability or acceptance that ear piercings perhaps have. A 2001 survey of attitudes toward tattoos found 67 percent of the respondents labeling those with body art "rebellious." Respondents also felt it was risky personally and professionally to have tattoos; 85 percent agreed that "People who have visible tattoos or body piercings should realize that this form of self-expression is likely to create obstacles in their career or personal relationships."

While men are judged negatively for tattoos, society is more accepting of tattoos on men than on women. Tattoos are seen as an expression of male gender; women who get a tattoo are considered to be violating gender rules and are therefore "a threat to social order," according to anthropologist Joy Ralph. Tattoos on men are seen as a break with conformity and a sign of independent thinking. When these same traits are applied to women, notes researcher Kathleen T. Doherty, they are evaluated much more harshly and negatively by society because women with tattoos refuse to obey norms concerning gender and women's appearance. If a woman does get tattooed, she is not judged as harshly if she has a small, delicate, and feminine tattoo, such as a flower or butterfly, or if it is not easily visible. But, according to Doherty, large or obviously "male" tattoos violate gender norms and make society uneasy.

Social attitudes toward body modification may be changing, however, since more women are getting tattoos and more men are getting pierced. The authors in *At Issue: Body Piercing and Tattoos* discuss the health risks of body modification and societal attitudes toward tattoos and piercings.

1

Body Piercing Can Be Done Safely

Association of Professional Piercers

The Association of Professional Piercers is an alliance of body piercing professionals dedicated to the dissemination of the most up-to-date information about body piercing.

Those who want a body piercing should use the services of a piercer who follows sterile procedures. All piercing studios should sterilize their piercing equipment with an autoclave. Piercers should also provide both oral and written guidelines detailing how to care for the piercing.

You have decided to have your body pierced and you are asking yourself, "I want it done now, so where do I go?" In this era of bloodborne diseases you *must* be very careful who you have perform your piercing! This guide is brought to you by the Association of Professional Piercers to assist you in making a better-informed decision regarding your piercing because **IT'S YOUR CHOICE!**

This is meant to be a guideline and to aid you in having a safe piercing experience.

See Their Autoclave (Sterlizer)

An autoclave is a device that sterilizes the jewelry, tools and equipment necessary to perform your piercing(s) by eliminating bacteria and its spores. The most effective units available

Association of Professional Piercers, "Choosing a Piercer," www.safepiercing.org, 2004.

to studios use a combination of steam and pressure. ("Dry Heat" is NOT considered appropriate for sterilization.) Absolutely no studio should be in operation without this vital piece of equipment!

The piercer should first wash and glove their hands.

A spore test (biological indicator) is the only way to know that an autoclave is working properly. Biological indicators actually test the autoclave's ability to kill even the most dangerous & resistant organisms such as HIV, Hepatitis, etc. The studio should keep recent results on file and be willing to show them to you.

Piercing Set-Up

Ask if you can watch them set-up for a piercing and be in the room when they set up for yours. The piercer should first wash and glove their hands. The equipment should be sealed in individual sterilized packages and placed on a tray. The piercer should change gloves if they touch anything in the room other than you and the sterile equipment. All needles should be in individual sterile packages and should be opened while you are present. NEVER let a piercer use a needle on you that was soaked in a liquid. All needles should be disposed of in a sharps container (usually a small red box marked "biohazard") after they have been used on a single client.

Aftercare Guidelines

The aftercare for your piercing should be explained to you and provided in writing. Read this sheet *before* you have the piercing done! If it tells you to treat your piercing with harsh soap, ointment, alcohol, or hydrogen peroxide, the studio is not keeping up with industry standards.

Piercers

Don't be misled into believing piercing is easy. It takes time and dedication to acquire the ability to correctly place and skillfully perform piercings. Piercers either serve an apprenticeship or are self-taught. Apprenticeships will generally last from 6 months to two years. Those who are self-taught will ideally have sought guidance from others in the field. Continued education is the hallmark of any conscientious piercer. It is perfectly acceptable and advisable to inquire about how long your piercer has been piercing, how they learned to pierce, and what they have done to keep their knowledge base current, i.e., courses on Anatomy, Aftercare, Aseptic Technique, etc.

The Studio

Are the walls washed and the carpet vacuumed? Is the staff bathed and neat? Is the restroom kept clean and tidy? Ideally, studios should have 5 separate areas: the counter, waiting room, piercing room(s), bathroom, and a separate sterilization room.

In most cases a license to operate means that the studio meets minimum requirements and has passed some sort of inspection. To find out if your area has established standards and inspections, call your local Health Department. If a studio is operating unlicensed in an area where licenses are required, report them to your local health department or city business license division.

Don't act impulsively or be swayed by a low price.

Look at their piercing photo portfolio. Are piercings placed to accent the anatomy or do they look awkward and poorly matched to the individual? If the portfolio features unusual looking placements, are there pictures of healed piercings, showing the actual viability of the placement?

Age Requirements

Regardless of any local legislation being more lenient, the following is an appropriate minimum standards policy on piercing minors: For any piercing of a minor, a parent or legal guardian must be present to sign a consent form. Proof positive, state issued photo identification is required from the legal guardian, and a bona fide form of identification from the minor. In the event the parent has a different last name and/or address from the child, court documentation is needed to prove the relationship, i.e., divorce papers, or a remarriage certificate. Under no circumstances is it acceptable or appropriate for a piercer to perform piercing on the nipples or genitals of an individual under 18 years of age.

Ear Piercing Guns

A number of states have made it illegal to use a gun on body piercings and with good reason. Most ear guns can't be sterilized in an autoclave and therefore don't meet the criteria for APP piercers' use of sterile disposable equipment.

Use Your Instincts

If you don't feel comfortable with the studio or the piercer you should leave. "I should have listened to my gut feeling" is something you should never have to say.

Don't act impulsively or be swayed by a low price. You generally get what you pay for (but some unskilled piercers charge plenty). Get referrals on a piercing shop/piercer from knowledgeable friends and/or the local health department....

Although individual studio requirements vary, most will expect you to:

Bring valid photo identification

Be completely sober

Be bathed with hair trimmed or tied back (where applicable)

Have eaten within 4 hours

If you are getting a genital or nipple piercing wear suitable, clean underwear/garments/bras

If possible, avoid Aspirin or other blood thinners

Have considered any potential health issues (i.e., individuals who require antibiotics prior to dental work should see their doctor prior to being pierced)

Studio Etiquette

At the counter: Don't handle your piercings (even if they are healed) as you may spread bacteria to the studio's common areas thereby endangering both staff and fellow patrons. Bring worn jewelry in a baggie or other sealed container. Never place worn jewelry on the counter or display.

In the restroom: Don't handle your piercings (see above). It is never appropriate to change your jewelry in the restroom or other locations in the studio.

If you want your jewelry changed at the studio, it should be done by one of the piercers, in the piercing room.

In the piercing room: Allow your piercer to direct you to an area where personal belongings may be placed *before* setting anything down.

Camera flashes can be very distracting during the performance of a piercing.

Check with your piercer before taking pictures.

Turn off your cell phone.

Dirty (unwashed) hands are the worst enemy for piercings.

Shopping for Jewelry

When referring to size of jewelry there are two measurements. One is the width (of a ring) or length (of a bar) called the "diameter" of the jewelry.

The other is the thickness of the jewelry, which is the "gauge." The smaller the gauge numbers the thicker the jewelry.

Generally speaking it is advisable to purchase your jewelry at the time of the piercing. Your piercer will need to select the jewelry best suited to your anatomy. Many studios will not insert jewelry purchased elsewhere in either a fresh or healed piercing as quality can not be verified. If the piercer insists on a certain style or size because that is the only item they have in stock, consider being pierced in a studio with a larger inventory.

Taking Care of Your Piercing

The best aftercare will depend on various factors. Each body is unique and every piercing is different. There are a number of things you can do to help your body to heal your piercing. Some of them are:

Keep your hands off the piercing! Dirty (unwashed) hands are the worst enemy for piercings. During the course of a day your hands become covered with germs. If you touch the piercing, even just near the area, you will deposit bacteria at the piercing site, possibly causing an infection.

Eating Correctly: It is a proven fact that if you eat a healthful, balanced diet your body functions better and heals faster. In most cases, taking vitamin C and zinc will promote healing.

Sea Salt: Applying a very mild, warm sea salt water soak (saline) to your piercing can help your body to heal your piercing. It may also reduce the risk of an infection by helping remove bacteria from the area.

Liquid Soap: It is widely accepted that a mild liquid soap used to gently wash the piercing followed by thorough rinsing is suitable for most piercings. Ask your piercer for suggestions on products that are available in your area. Usually once or twice a day works best; don't overclean the piercing. Also, don't use multiple cleaners at the same time. (Soap plus sea salt water is ok.)

NEVER use the following:

Hydrogen Peroxide or Alcohol: Over the years piercing industry professionals have learned that these products are far too strong and cause more problems than they help.

Antibiotic ointments, gels and creams: These products trap dirt and germs inside a piercing and prevent oxygen from reaching the wound. They may work well for cuts and scrapes but are not good for piercings.

2

Body Piercing Has Health Risks

Dana Slagle

Teen Vogue *is a fashion magazine geared toward teenagers.*

Many teenagers and young adults consider body piercings as just another fashion accessory. However, body piercings have significan health risks. Piercings are often ripped or torn, and they can cause disfiguration as well as infection and large and unsightly scars. People should think twice about getting pierced.

Ashley was intrigued when she saw her friend with this thing bobbing around in her mouth. It wasn't long before she followed her classmate's example and got two piercings: a tongue ring and a navel ring. "With glow-in-the-dark balls, your tongue can glow in a club!" she explains. But after swallowing the ball on her tongue ring and developing an infection around her navel ring (it kept getting caught on her jeans), she realized that piercings were more hassle than they were worth.

Nowadays, it's not just club-hoppers like the Toronto-based Ashley (now 23) getting pierced. Stella [whose name has been changed], seventeen, a Los Angeles native, sees her piercings as another fashion accessory and has amassed nine. Jamie [whose name has been changed], an eighteen-year-old, has eleven piercings so far, and doesn't consider them to be a big deal. Plenty of other teens seem to feel the same way: A Mayo Clinic study done at Pace University in Pleasantville, New

York, found that 60 percent of the female college students who participated had body or facial piercings (other than the standard earlobes).

But while they may seem cool, piercing comes with significant risks. Gerald Imber, M.D., a New York City-based plastic surgeon, regularly sees disfigurations from it. "Patients come in with ripped earlobes from earrings being torn out," he says. "If a tongue ring gets ripped out, it's a bloodbath." Jamie's run-in with her piercings was similarly painful. "My navel ring got caught on the buttonholes on the bottom of my shirt. Then, the same thing happened with my eyebrow ring. But no regrets they're not like tattoos, which you can't take back."

Unfortunately for Jamie, the evidence differs. An allergic reaction can cause skin to pick up the stud's color, leaving a permanent black ring around the piercing like a tattoo, notes Imber. Piercing also becomes irreversible if scars develop or holes don't close up (which is common with eyebrow rings). While lobes heal in about a month, cartilage can take up to a year and is prone to infections. As Robert Guida, M.D., a New York City-based plastic surgeon, explains, "Over the last ten years, the incidence of auricular perichondritis [an infection of the skin, soft tissue, and cartilage] from piercing has doubled. This can result in 'cauliflower ear,' where the ear loses its shape and is permanently deformed."

If you're serious about getting pierced and have your parents' blessing (most states mandate parental consent if you're under eighteen or 21), go to someone approved by the Association of Professional Piercers, which has rigorous requirements for membership. Daniel Hindle, a seventeen-year-old teen from England, died after receiving a lip piercing. The suspected cause? Blood poisoning, from an infection due to piercing. Think twice, cautions Roy Geronemus, M.D., a dermasurgeon in New York City: "It's unnecessary to risk deforming yourself when there are other ways to express your personality, like through clothing. Most people get sick of their piercings by college anyway. Is it really worth it?"

3

Tattoos Can Be Done Safely

Alliance of Professional Tattooists

The Alliance of Professional Tattooists is an educational organization that addresses the health and safety issues facing the tattoo industry.

Tattoo artists are increasingly aware of the potential risks associated with getting a tattoo and have established standard precautions to reduce the risks. Tattoo equipment is sterilized, and the artists use sterile gloves and single-use equipment, including ink and lubricant. The tattoo artist should answer any questions posed about procedure.

The last ten years have seen an educational renaissance within the tattoo industry. Artists have become increasingly aware of the potential risks associated with bloodborne pathogens and have taken steps to protect their clients and themselves. With just a little education and some research, you can assure yourself of a safe, professional tattoo.

Blood-borne Diseases

Will I get HIV or AIDS? HIV is a very delicate virus and does not survive long outside the human body. Nor is it spread through casual contact. Generally, the virus is only transmitted when sufficient quantities of highly infected blood are introduced into the body of another. The structure of tattoo needles does not lend itself to HIV transmission. According to the Centers for Disease Control in Atlanta, there has never

Alliance of Professional Tattooists, "Frequently Asked Questions," www.safe-tattoos .com. Reproduced by permission.

been a case of HIV transmission from tattooing in the United States. Cases outside the US were not positively attributed to tattooing because all reported cases also fit the profile of a "high risk" lifestyle.

What about Hepatitis? The disease to consider when getting tattooed is hepatitis. Hepatitis, unlike HIV, is a very hardy virus that can survive long periods outside the human body and can be transmitted through little more than a scratch with an infected needle. To combat this and any other infectious bloodborne pathogen, artists autoclave their single-service equipment, use individual portions of ink and lubricant, dispose of used sharps according to OSHA [Occupational Safety and Health Administration] guidelines, use EPA [Environmental Protection Agency]-registered virucidals to clean their stations between clients, and use barrier protection. These procedures are called Standard Precautions. Basically, the artist must treat everyone (including themselves) as though they were infectious. That way, everyone is protected and the potential for infection is reduced to next to nothing.

An autoclave is the only acceptable means of equipment sterilization in the tattoo shop.

Choosing an Artist

How should I pick an artist? APT [Alliance of Professional Tattooists] admits artists based on their desire to educate themselves in safe tattoo procedure rather than artistic merit. For that reason, we do not recommend specific artists. Not to mention, there are a number of excellent artists who, for whatever reason, have not joined APT. While we would like you to patronize one of our artists, it would be a shame to pass up an excellent artist simply because they did not belong to our organization. You can still assure yourself that you are in good hands by following a few simple guidelines.

Your concerns are twofold. You need to find an artist whose work you like, who will work on you safely. Ask people where they got tattooed, especially if you really like the work you see. Ask to see photographs of the artist's work. Most often, the pictures will have been taken right after the work was completed, so redness and swelling are common. In spite of that, there are things you can learn. Are the lines clean and smooth or broken and jagged? Do they meet up? Does the artist work in the style you are looking for? Taking time to check out a few artists and shops will ensure that you are happy with your results.

At the Shop

Make sure the shop is neat and clean. What you see in the front room is a pretty good indication of what you will see elsewhere in the shop. Ask questions about the shop's safety procedures. What are they doing to ensure your health and well-being? The personnel should be willing and able to answer your questions. If you feel they are brushing your concerns aside or can't answer you, leave and seek out a *professional* shop.

The Equipment

What is single-service equipment? All equipment should be single service. This means that each needle and tube set is individually packaged, dated and sealed and autoclaved. The artist should open a fresh set of needles and tubes in front of you. Any ointments, pigments, needles, gloves, razors, plastic trays or containers used in applying your new tattoo are discarded after use. After the tattoo application, the artist will disinfect the work area with an EPA-approved virucidal that will kill any surface bacteria or viruses.

What is an autoclave? An autoclave is the only acceptable means of equipment sterilization in the tattoo shop. It is a machine that uses a combination of heat, steam and pressure to kill all pathogenic microorganisms known to man. If the shop does not use an autoclave, do not get tattooed there. Shops should keep regular records of their autoclave use and testing. Ask to see them if you feel uncertain.

Why does the artist wear gloves? Your artist should be wearing gloves any time they are touching broken skin and should change their gloves regularly. This protects both you and the artist from any bloodborne pathogens that may be present.

What to Expect

This is my first tattoo. What should I expect? Getting your first tattoo can be a very exciting experience and being prepared for what to expect can keep it fun. First, you should be well rested and well fed. If you are tired, or your blood sugar is low, you may experience a higher level of discomfort than you normally would. Drinking alcohol before getting tattooed is always a bad idea. Not only do you become dehydrated, it will also cause you to bleed more and consequently have a negative effect on your new tattoo.

There will be blood. The amount varies from person to person, but usually it is about what you would expect from a scraped knee or rug burn. The level of pain also varies from person to person, but most people don't find it unbearable. The best thing to do is just accept the discomfort and relax. Fighting or tensing will only increase your discomfort.

If you start to feel faint or a little "green," tell your artist right away instead of toughing it out. There is absolutely nothing wrong with taking a break. Your artist is prepared for this sort of thing and knows how to handle it.

If you need to change position or stretch, go to the bathroom, sneeze or wiggle for any reason, let your artist know *before* you do it.

Your new tattoo will get a patch of shiny skin over it or it may scab over. Leave the scab alone! This is a normal part of the healing process. Picking the scab may lead to infection or damage to your tattoo. The scab will slough off gradually in the course of a week or two. If you have any questions during the healing process, call your artist. Don't rely on stories told to you by your friends.

4

Tattooing Has Health Risks

U.S. Food & Drug Administration

The U.S. Food & Drug Administration is a federal agency that oversees and enforces public health laws. Among its responsibilities is ensuring that tattoo inks and cosmetics are safe for human skin.

The primary complications from getting a tattoo include infections, allergic reactions to the ink, and scarring. Some inks are not compatible with magnetic resonance imaging, which may cause problems if a doctor orders one for a tattooed patient. The most common problem with tattoos is that many people become dissatisfied with the tattoo due to a faded or blurred image. Removing a tattoo is a painstaking process and expensive. Temporary tattoos and henna dyes may be an acceptable substitute for permanent tattoos, but not all dyes are approved for use on human skin.

FDA [Food and Drug Administration] considers the inks used in intradermal tattoos, including permanent makeup, to be cosmetics and considers the pigments used in the inks to be color additives requiring premarket approval under the Federal Food, Drug, and Cosmetic Act. However, because of other public health priorities and a previous lack of evidence of safety concerns, FDA has not traditionally regulated tattoo inks or the pigments used in them. The actual practice of tattooing is regulated by local jurisdictions. FDA is aware of more than 150 reports of adverse reactions in consumers to

U.S. Food & Drug Administration, "Tattoos and Permanent Makeup," www.cfsan.fda .gov, July 14, 2006. Reproduced by permission.

certain permanent make-up ink shades, and it is possible that the actual number of women affected was greater. In addition, concerns raised by the scientific community regarding the pigments used in these inks have prompted FDA to investigate the safe use of tattoo inks. FDA continues [as of 2006] to evaluate the extent and severity of adverse events associated with tattooing and is conducting research on inks. As new information is assessed, the agency will consider whether additional actions are necessary to protect public health.

Other Areas of Concern

In addition to the reported adverse reactions, areas of concern include tattoo removal, infections that result from tattooing, and the increasing variety of pigments and diluents being used in tattooing. More than fifty different pigments and shades are in use, and the list continues to grow. Although a number of color additives are approved for use in cosmetics, none is approved for injection into the skin. Using an unapproved color additive in a tattoo ink makes the ink adulterated. Many pigments used in tattoo inks are not approved for skin contact at all. Some are industrial grade colors that are suitable for printers' ink or automobile paint.

Nevertheless, many individuals choose to undergo tattooing in its various forms. For some, it is an aesthetic choice or an initiation rite. Some choose permanent makeup as a time saver or because they have physical difficulty applying regular, temporary makeup. For others, tattooing is an adjunct to reconstructive surgery, particularly of the face or breast, to simulate natural pigmentation. People who have lost their eyebrows due to alopecia (a form of hair loss) may choose to have "eyebrows" tattooed on, while people with vitiligo (a lack of pigmentation in areas of the skin) may try tattooing to help camouflage the condition.

Whatever their reason, consumers should be aware of the risks involved in order to make an informed decision.

What Risks Are Involved in Tattooing?

The following are the primary complications that can result from tattooing:

- *Infection.* Unsterile tattooing equipment and needles can transmit infectious diseases, such as hepatitis and skin infections caused by *Staphylococcus aureus* ("staph") bacteria. Tattoos received at facilities not regulated by your state or at facilities that use unsterile equipment (or re-use ink) may prevent you from being accepted as a blood or plasma donor for twelve months.

- *Removal problems.* Despite advances in laser technology, removing a tattoo is a painstaking process, usually involving several treatments and considerable expense. Complete removal without scarring may be impossible.

- *Allergic reactions.* Although FDA has received reports of numerous adverse ractions associated with certain shades of ink in permanent makeup, marketed by a particular manufacturer, reports of allergic reactions to tattoo pigments have been rare. However, when they happen they may be particularly troublesome because the pigments can be hard to remove. Occasionally, people may develop an allergic reaction to tattoos they have had for years.

- *Granulomas.* These are nodules that may form around material that the body perceives as foreign, such as particles of tattoo pigment.

- *Keloid formation.* If you are prone to developing keloids—scars that grow beyond normal boundaries—you are at risk of keloid formation from a tattoo. Keloids may form any time you injure or traumatize your skin. *Micropigmentation: State of the Art*, a book written by

Charles Zwerling, M.D., Annette Walker, R.N., and Norman Goldstein, M.D., states that keloids occur more frequently as a consequence of tattoo removal.

Complications from MRIs

- *MRI complications.* There have been reports of people with tattoos or permanent makeup who experienced swelling or burning in the affected areas when they underwent magnetic resonance imaging (MRI). This seems to occur only rarely and apparently without lasting effects.

There also have been reports of tattoo pigments interfering with the quality of the image. This seems to occur mainly when a person with permanent eyeliner undergoes MRI of the eyes. Mascara may produce a similar effect. The difference is that mascara is easily removable.

The cause of these complications is uncertain. Some have theorized that they result from an interaction with the metallic components of some pigments.

However, the risks of avoiding an MRI when your doctor has recommended one are likely to be much greater than the risks of complications from an interaction between the MRI and tattoo or permanent makeup. Instead of avoiding an MRI, individuals who have tattoos or permanent makeup should inform the radiologist or technician of this fact in order to take appropriate precautions and avoid complications.

A Common Problem: Dissatisfaction

A common problem that may develop with tattoos is the desire to remove them. Removing tattoos and permanent makeup can be very difficult.

Although tattoos may be satisfactory at first, they sometimes fade. Also, if the tattooist injects the pigments too deeply into the skin, the pigments may migrate beyond the original sites, resulting in a blurred appearance.

Another cause of dissatisfaction is that the human body changes over time, and styles change with the season. The permanent makeup that may have looked flattering when first injected may later clash with changing skin tones and facial or body contours. People who plan to have facial cosmetic surgery are advised that the appearance of their permanent makeup may become distorted. The tattoo that seemed stylish at first may become dated and embarrassing. And changing tattoos or permanent makeup is not as easy as changing your mind. . . .

What About Temporary Tattoos?

Temporary tattoos, such as those applied to the skin with a moistened wad of cotton, fade several days after application. Most contain color additives approved for cosmetic use on the skin. However, the agency has issued an import alert for certain foreign-made temporary tattoos.

The temporary tattoos subject to the import alert are not allowed into the United States because they don't carry the FDA-mandated ingredient labels or they contain colors not permitted by FDA for use in cosmetics applied to the skin. FDA has received reports of allergic reactions to temporary tattoos.

In a similar action, FDA has issued an import alert for henna intended for use on the skin. Henna is approved only for use as a hair dye, not for direct application to the skin. Also, henna typically produces a reddish brown tint, raising questions about what ingredients are added to produce the varieties of colors labeled as "henna," such as "black henna" and "blue henna." FDA has also received reports of allergic reactions to products applied to the skin that contain henna.

5

The Threat of Suicide from Tongue Piercing Is Exaggerated

James Weber

James Weber, the medical liaison for the Association of Professional Piercers and the editor of The Point: The Quarterly Journal of the Association of Professional Piercers, *owns a body piercing shop in Philadelphia.*

Trigeminal neuralgia (TN) is a condition characterized by sudden and intense pain caused by pressure on the trigeminal nerve, which is responsible for sensation in the face. Many people afflicted with typical trigeminal neuralgia commit suicide because pain medication does not alleviate the pain. While people with atypical TN experience severe pain, it is not as debilitating as typical TN. Trigeminal neuralgia is an extremely rare condition and even more rare among people with piercings.

When I got into work on Friday, October 20th, 2006, there was a fax waiting for me. It was a copy of a newspaper article from the *San Francisco Daily* with a headline that read, "Tongue Piercing Tied to Painful 'Suicide Disease.'" I knew it was going to be a busy weekend.

And then the calls started. Had I seen the articles? Had I read them? What was I, as the Medical Liaison for the Association of Professional Piercers, going to do about them?

Since the article originated at the Associated Press, it was everywhere. (The AP news service is the oldest and largest news organization in the world. It supplies news to over 1,700 US newspapers daily, 5,000 TV and radio stations, and 8,500 international subscribers.) The piece was printed in dozens of newspapers, occasionally with different headlines over the same body provided by the Associated Press.

The Gist of the Article

For those that haven't seen the article, the gist of it is this:

A research letter written up in the *Journal of the American Medical Association (JAMA)*, and published on October 18th, 2006, was titled "Atypical Trigeminal Neuralgia Associated with Tongue Piercing." It outlines the case of an Italian woman who complained of face and head pain that started one month after she had her tongue pierced and lasted for two months until she removed her jewelry. In the article, the pain was purported to come in episodes "described as 'electric shocks'" which "lasted from 10 to 30 seconds, and recurred 20 to 30 times each day, increasing in frequency and severity in the latter weeks." According to the authors, these episodes were consistent with the disorder known as trigeminal neuralgia.

Trigeminal Neuralgia

Trigeminal neuralgia is a condition characterized by sudden attacks of pain involving different sections of the face. These attacks are severe, and are usually described as resembling electric shocks—the pain is intermittent, but intense. And, most importantly, the article goes on to describe several types of trigeminal neuralgia, the main two being *typical* trigeminal neuralgia, and *atypical* trigeminal neuralgia.

Typical trigeminal neuralgia is incredibly painful, and most often caused by an enlarged blood vessel putting pressure on the trigeminal nerve root (the trigeminal nerve is one of twelve cranial nerves serving the face and head). What results from this pressure is an extreme, electric shock-like pain that is completely debilitating for the sufferer. (The diagnosis of typical TN is based in part upon the sufferer's description of his/her pain.)

Atypical trigeminal neuralgia is a less common form of the disorder and is characterized by less intense, constant, dull burning or aching pain, often with occasional electric shock-like stabs. Atypical TN is also commonly treatable with medications used for typical TN, such as carbamazapine. (It should be noted that, in the *JAMA* article, the patient was treated with carbamazapine with little effect.)

While the title of the . . . article—"Tongue Piercing Linked to Pain"—was not especially inflammatory, things got worse each time the article was reprinted.

The woman in the *JAMA* article was diagnosed with atypical trigeminal neuralgia, based on the description of her pain (and her lack of reaction to the carbamazapine). After the failure of the medication, she took out her tongue piercing jewelry, and the symptoms disappeared completely within 48 hours. Though it was speculated that the tongue piercing was the cause of the TN, it was noted, "The symptom was probably secondary to a lingual metallic implant, and although findings indicate the involvement of the trigeminal system, the location of the piercing and implant should not have resulted in trigeminal injury." It further references an article in the *New England Journal of Medicine*, where a 66-year-old woman was suffering from trigeminal neuralgia from a mercury-amalgam filling in one tooth coming in contact with a gold crown on the adjacent one. On the whole, the research letter in *JAMA* was informative, well written and, above all, objective. The same cannot be said about the Associated Press article.

Biased and Slanted Reporting

The problem with the AP article was that it failed to differentiate between *typical* trigeminal neuralgia and *atypical* trigeminal neuralgia. It also was the first mention of TN's most unfortunate nickname: the suicide disease. Because of the overwhelmingly intense pain, those suffering from typical TN have a very high incidence of suicide—the pain is so horrible that many feel this is the only way out. This is not true of atypical TN, which is a much more minor, and more manageable form of the disorder. The combination of these two pieces of the AP article—the lack of distinction between typical and atypical TN, and the inclusion of the phrase "suicide disease"—set the stage for the press that followed.

Piercers and other body modification artists . . . [are] the whipping boy for traditional news services because . . . [we're] not insisting that news outlets are held accountable for misinformation and exaggerations that are printed about us and what we do.

While the title of the AP article—"Tongue Piercing Linked to Pain"—was not especially inflammatory, things got worse each time the article was reprinted. Each news posting (print or Web) provided their own headlines, and made decisions about how much of the article to reprint. (Many papers chose to edit the article for length, often leaving out the paragraph where Dr. Marcelo Galarza, an author of the original study states, "Certainly, this was an isolated case, an extremely rare complication of this kind of piercing.") This is where the incitive headlines appeared, such as the one [on] MSNBC, which screamed "Teen's Tongue Piercing Causes 'Suicide Disease.'"

The Scapegoat

Strangely, the whole incident reminded me of *The Simpsons*. (Yes, the TV show.) On the first season's DVD collection, if you listen to the writers' commentary during the episodes, you hear them often mention the cheap shots and cruel jokes included at the expense of the old. This was because every week they were pitted against *The Cosby Show* in their time bracket. And while *The Simpsons* led the ratings with the younger demographic, anyone over 40 that was watching TV at that time was watching Bill Cosby and his TV family. This gave the creative team at *The Simpsons* free rein to make the elderly the butt of any joke they wanted—there was simply no one watching who would complain to the network.

This is much the same way piercers and other body modification artists allow themselves to be portrayed [in] the mainstream media: We're the whipping boy for traditional news services because not only are we a marginalized and unorganized group, but we're simply not watching, and not insisting that news outlets are held accountable for misinformation and exaggerations that are printed about us and what we do.

Taking Action

So what was I going to do about the mess started by the Associated Press?

The first thing I did was to write a letter on behalf of the APP to the Associated Press writer, politely seeking to educate her on the situation, and explaining my interest as the APP's Medical Liaison.

The next, more daunting task was to attempt to send a letter to the editor of every news outlet that ran the AP article. After emailing out the first round of letters for the articles that were already sent me, I composed a letter to the APP membership asking for help in tracking down versions of the article in all media. This message was sent to every APP member via email asking each to forward me contact info for any paper they encountered which printed the AP story—which quite a few did. (I then sent out the letter to each news source.)

This request was also posted on MySpace, and I saw the letter re-posted repeatedly in bulletins boards over the course of several days.

The response to all this was amazing. I received emails from members (and non-members) from all over the country. These included about fifty links to outlets running the AP letter, from newspapers to TV stations to radio stations to Internet news groups. I spent a day modifying the letter template, and composing and sending a letter to each news editor. I posted on newspaper and newsgroup comment boards, and on larger papers that listed postal addresses, I had letters printed and sent from the APP office to each of the newspapers.

We Can Make a Difference

At times it did seem rather futile. How many of my letters to the editors did I think would actually get printed? It didn't matter—I was simply determined to not let tongue piercing be the focus of yet another misinformed, sensationalistic attack on what we do, on what we hold to be most important.

And it must have worked. The last time I did a Google search with the words "tongue piercing suicide disease," my letter came up #3, on the *Chicago Tribune*'s Web site. Not too bad.

And while we are still a long way, as an industry, from getting the respect that we deserve, we don't have to be passive participants in the process. If we don't like the way we're being portrayed by the mainstream media, we have a responsibility to our industry and ourselves to try to do something about it. Change will be slow to come, but I believe that, unified and organized, we can make a difference.

6

Tongue Piercing Is Linked to "Suicide Disease"

Brendan Quealy

As of 2007, Brendan Quealy is the online editor for the Flyer, *the newspaper for Lewis University in Romeoville, Illinois.*

A woman who experienced stabbing pains in her face was diagnosed with a disorder sometimes called "suicide disease" because its sufferers believe suicide is the only way they can get relief from the pain. But once the woman removed the metal stud jewelry from her tongue, the pain disappeared. Although the woman's case is a rare complication of tongue piercing, it has been added to the list of risks associated with piercing.

Is it possible for a piece of metal, just slightly larger than an inch, to cause what is universally considered the "most painful affliction known to medical practice?" According to 21-year-old Stefania Fraccalvieri and her doctors, not only is it possible, but it is in fact a reality.

Excruciating Pain

Two years ago [in 2004] just days after getting her tongue pierced with a metal stud, Fraccalvieri began to experience what she describes as "excruciating, stabbing pain attacks" in her face and neck. These attacks struck 20 to 30 times a day, at random points, and lasted anywhere between 10 and 30 seconds each.

Brendan Quealy, "Surprising Side Effect," *The Flyer*, November 24, 2006. Reproduced by permission of the author.

After being taken to the emergency room and seen by a doctor, she was diagnosed with trigeminal neuralgia, or better known in layman's terms as 'suicide disease'. It is referred to by this name because of the effect that trigeminal neuralgia has on the mental well-being of the person afflicted, causing such severe depression that some opt to take their own lives as a means to deal with the pain.

While Fraccalvieri's doctors tried, without success, to alleviate her pain through the use of painkillers, anti-depressants, and anti-convulsants, the only treatment that worked was the removal of her tongue piercing.

As it turns out, the tongue piercing was irritating Fraccalvieri's fifth cranial (trigeminal) nerve, which branches out to the lower jaw and is connected to the tongue. Because of this irritation, she experienced episodes of intense and "electrical shock-like" pain in the areas of her face connected to the nerve.

Added to List of Complications

Because this was just the first reported case of trigeminal neuralgia caused by a tongue piercing, the *Journal of the American Medical Association* (JAMA) was hesitant to add it as a risk until further studies could be conducted. Last month [October 2006] after two years of research and corresponding resistance from the Association of Professional Piercers (APP), trigeminal neuralgia has been included in the risks of tongue piercing, right alongside risks like tetanus, heart infections, brain abscesses, chipped teeth and receding gums.

"I never realized just how dangerous it could be," says Ray Dreisen, a 20-year-old residential construction worker who had his tongue pierced sophomore year in high school. "I know they explained the complications to me, but I was already set on getting it done."

Ellen Hanos, a registered nurse at Christ Hospital in Oak Lawn, [Illinois], explains why a tongue piercing can cause so many complications: "The tongue is a rather dangerous area of the body to be pierced because it has so many blood vessels that increase the risk of an infection spreading to the major organs and the nervous system."

A spokesperson for the APP still trying to fight the ruling says, "It is extremely rare (occurring in about one of 15 thousand people), and it is wrong to frighten people away from something they want to do." Even so, the American Medical Association still feels it is their responsibility to warn of any possible dangers, especially because so few people are familiar with the condition.

The Piercing Waiver Form

The only change to the piercing procedure will be an addition made to the risks portion of the waiver form that is signed before someone can get pierced. This begs two questions: Is this enough? Do people actually read the waiver before they sign it?

"I skimmed over it before I got my nose pierced," says Lewis University student and Education major Jacki Griebel. "I really just paid more attention to how they told me to clean it."

While some skim over the waiver, others like Jamie LaFevers, a Psychology major at Lewis, read it from top to bottom. "What I found really interesting was how long it was compared to the waiver I signed to get my tattoo. The tattoo one was only about a paragraph long, but to get my ear pierced I had to read four pages."

While both Griebel and LaFevers admitted that they have never had any interest in getting their tongues pierced, after learning about this possible side effect, they were even more turned off by the idea. "No, I just couldn't imagine doing that now," says Griebel, "I would even tell my friends not to do it. It just seems too painful and I don't think it's worth it." Her sentiment would certainly be shared by Stefania Fraccalvieri.

7

Piercings and Tattoos Are Linked to Suicides

Bruce Jancin

Bruce Jancin is a reporter for Clinical Psychiatry News.

A survey of more than 4,700 teens and adults who participate in body modification—tattoos, piercing, and/or scarification—found that two-thirds of them had considered or attempted suicide. The location and type of body modification were correlated with the likelihood of attempting or considering suicide. Nine piercing sites and nine tattoo sites were associated with high rates of suicide attempts. Some of the highest rates of suicidality were found among those who participate in scarification.

Body modification enthusiasts—individuals who undergo piercing, tattooing, and/or scarification—have a high rate of self-reported prior suicide attempts, David Lester, Ph.D, said at the [2005] conference of the American Association of Suicidology.

An Intriguing Question

This observation from a large cross-sectional study of body art aficionados raises an intriguing question: Is body modification a marker for increased risk of suicidality, or is it instead a sort of substitute activity?

"As body modification is now becoming socially acceptable, maybe it's something that high-risk adolescents could do to reduce their suicidality. Of course, that's a question that would require a longitudinal controlled study to properly answer," noted Dr. Lester, professor of psychology at Richard Stockton College of New Jersey, Pomona.

A detailed survey of some 4,700 individuals who frequent a Web site devoted to hard-core body modification . . . concluded that only 34% had never considered suicide. Thirty-nine percent indicated they had only contemplated it, and 27% had made one or more attempts.

"That strikes me as high," Dr. Lester commented.

Of 25 possible anatomic sites for piercing, 9 were associated with increased suicidality.

The median age of respondents to the survey was 21 years. Eighty-eight percent were white, and roughly 45% were students. Fifty-six percent of the body modification enthusiasts described themselves as heterosexual, 38% as bisexual, and only 5% as homosexual.

Body Modification Related to Suicide History

The type of body modification procedure individuals had undergone appeared to be related to their suicidality history. So did the anatomic site they selected for alteration.

For example, 27% of men and 46% of women with a pierced eyebrow—a relatively common form of body modification—reported that they had previously attempted suicide, compared with 18% of men and 32% of women without an eyebrow piercing, Dr. Lester said.

Twenty-four percent of men with a tongue piercing reported previously attempting suicide, compared with 18% of those without this body modification. Given the very large sample size, that difference is highly statistically significant, he said at the meeting.

Similarly, 37% of women with a pierced tongue reported prior deliberate self-harm, compared with 30% without a pierced tongue.

Altogether, of 25 possible anatomic sites for piercing, 9 were associated with increased suicidality.

Tattoos at nine specific anatomic sites were associated with an increase in self-reported suicide attempts. "I would have predicted a lesser association with suicidality, given how much more popular tattoos have become since several decades ago, when they were viewed as deviant," Dr. Lester observed.

Scarification

Some of the highest rates of suicidality were found among individuals who engaged in scarification. For example, 39% of men and 48% of women with scarification of the upper arm or shoulder reported one or more prior attempts at suicide, compared with 18% and 32%, respectively, without this particular body modification.

Frequenters of a Web site devoted to body modification constitute a rather skewed survey population. As a sort of quick-and-dirty assessment of the survey's reliability, Dr. Lester checked to see if three well-established associations in the suicidology literature held true among respondents to the body modification survey.

All three rang true among the body modification crowd: female respondents reported more suicidality than males, heterosexuals reported less extensive suicidality histories than homosexuals or bisexuals, and individuals who said they have been depressed were more likely to report prior attempts at suicide.

8

Piercing Is Linked with Risky Behaviors Among Teens

Joan-Carles Suris, Andre Jeannin, Isabelle Chossis, and Pierre-Andre Michaud

Joan-Carles Suris, Isabelle Chossis, and Pierre-Andre Michaud are physicians and researchers with the Research Group on Adolescent Health at the University Institute of Social and Preventive Medicine in Lausanne, Switzerland. Andre Jeannin is with the Multidisciplinary Unit for Adolescent Health at UISPM.

A study of Swiss adolescents found that multiple piercings are a marker for risk behaviors such as substance abuse, risky sexual behaviors, suicide, school truancy, and other delinquent behavior. The study's prevalence rates are similar to those found among adolescents and young adults in North America. Pierced adolescents are more likely to be risk-takers.

B ody piercing among young people has been linked with risk behaviors such as the abuse of legal and illegal substances, risky sexual behavior, school truancy and running away, suicide ideation and attempts, and delinquent behavior.

Body art and, more specifically, piercing, is becoming normative among adolescents, with prevalence close to 70% in some studies. However, studies of adolescents are few, and most used local or convenience samples or populations known to be at high risk, such as detainees. To date [as of 2007], the only population-based study among adolescents reported a prevalence rate of 7.2% among females and 1.5% among males.

Objectives of the Study

Our objectives:

- to ascertain the prevalence of piercing among a nationally representative sample of adolescents

- to assess whether a piercing is a marker for risk behaviors

- to assess whether having more than one piercing is a cumulative marker for risk behaviors

- Implications

A Starting Point for Discussion

Our results indicate that body piercing (other than earlobes) is a marker for risk behaviors, and that, among females, multiple piercing seems to be a cumulative marker. We should pay particular attention to potential harmful behaviors among these adolescents. We should not stigmatize pierced adolescents. Body art is more than just an indicator of deviancy. In other words, as all adolescents should be screened for risky behaviors, this specific population offers the advantage of piercing as a starting point for a discussion.

We found that body piercing is increasingly popular among adolescents in Switzerland, especially among females. Our prevalence rates are higher than those reported by T. A. Roberts et al., but (as they suggest) it may well be due to the societal trend, as their data were collected in 1996.

The Pierced and the Unpierced

Academic performance was the main sociodemographic difference between pierced and unpierced adolescents. As a marker of risk, piercing was negatively associated with academic performance, as found elsewhere regarding healthy behaviors. Like other studies, this sample exhibited increased drug use and risky sexual behavior, but no increase in suicide attempt.

Among females in our sample, more than 1 piercing is associated with having multiple sex partners and marijuana use. S.T. Carroll et al. also found that having multiple piercings was associated with illegal drug use. For males in our study, the only association with multiple piercings was an increase in suicide attempts.

From our results, it could be hypothesized that more than 1 piercing is a cumulative marker for some risk behaviors, mainly among females. Though associations for males were similar to those for females, the differences between pierced and unpierced groups did not reach statistical significance. However, the relatively small sample of pierced males discourages definitive conclusions.

Pierced adolescents were less satisfied with their bodies than their unpierced counterparts, though the difference is significant only for females.

Young people indicate that the main reasons they obtain a piercing are a sense of uniqueness or self-expression, with only one-fifth indicating that they obtain it for aesthetics only. As we did not assess the reasons to obtain a body piercing in this study, it could be that they had it done to increase their body satisfaction, that their body satisfaction was lower after having it done, or simply that they do not get pierced to increase their satisfaction with their body.

The Survey's Participants

Population. Data were drawn from the 2002 Swiss Multicenter Adolescent Survey on Health database, a survey of 7,548 students ages 16 to 20 years (3,658 of whom were female). In Switzerland, school is mandatory up to age 16. Afterwards, about 30% of adolescents follow to further high school, 60% go to vocational school as an apprentice (1 or 2 days of class per week and the rest spent at work), and 10% do not continue their education.

Classroom survey. The survey was an anonymous classroom questionnaire approved by the ethical committee of the Medicine Faculty in Lausanne.... Ninety-one subjects (1%) did not answer the question referring to body piercing and were excluded. The final sample had 7,457 subjects (3,628 females)....

In a second step, adolescents having one piercing were compared with those having more than one piercing, using the same method.

Overall, 20.2% of our sample had a piercing, and it was significantly more prevalent among females than males: 33.8% vs 7.4%

Single Piercing

Having a piercing was significantly associated with all the risk behavior variables both in males and females. In both genders, pierced adolescents were significantly older, more frequently on an apprentice academic track, perceived advanced puberty, not living with both parents, had felt depressed, and were sensation-seeking. Additionally, pierced females were less likely to be satisfied with their body, less likely to be foreign-born, and more likely to have a mother with low education (mandatory school or less)....

Controlling for all significant background variables, pierced females were more likely to have had multiple sexual partners, not to have used a condom at last intercourse, to be regular smokers, and to be current users of cannabis or other illegal drugs. Among males, all risk behavior variables remained significant, except suicide ideation and attempt.

Multiple Piercings

One-third (34.1%) of pierced subjects had more than 1 piercing, with similar rates for males (35.3%) and females (33.8%)....

Among females, having more than one piercing was associated with being an apprentice, perceived advanced puberty, parents not living together, sensation seeking, and being depressed. With the exception of condom use at last intercourse, they were significantly more likely to engage in all risky behaviors.

All published studies seem to indicate that pierced adolescents are more likely to be risk-taking.

For males, the only difference between single and multiple piercings was that the latter were more likely to have attempted suicide. . . .

The only variables associated with females having more than one piercing were having multiple sexual partners and using cannabis.

Limitations of This Study

The main strength of our study is that it is based on a nationally representative sample of adolescents. However, a few limitations need to be stressed.

The cross-sectional nature of our survey does not allow us to assess causality. The questionnaire was filled in the classroom, which excludes absentees and dropouts, both known to be at higher risk. Additionally, we do not know the location or the size of the piercings; some locations (e.g., nipples or genitalia) are more likely associated with risk behaviors.

Can These Results Be Generalized?

But to what extent can our results be generalized to other, non-European adolescent populations? The prevalence rate is similar to those found among North American adolescents and college students. All published studies seem to indicate that pierced adolescents are more likely to be risk-taking.

That would indicate that our results are on the right track. However, more population-based studies need to be done to fully confirm this.

9

Piercings Are Popular Among Teens

Meghan Bard

Meghan Bard is a reporter for the Sentinel and Enterprise *in Fitchburg, Massachusetts.*

Despite the fact that many parents do not approve of body piercings, more and more parents are giving their consent to allow their children to receive body piercings. Body piercings are becoming more mainstream and more accepted, and parents prefer that their children get pierced by professionals who use sterile techniques, than let them attempt to do it themselves and incur possible life-threatening infections.

B rittany Lassen got her nose pierced 4 months ago [April 2005] and she had her bellybutton pierced when she was 13.

"I've been into (piercings) since I was really little," said Lassen, 16, of Hubbardston [Massachussets].

Lassen said she had to convince her mother to go with her to Acute Body Arts in Quinebaug, Conn., where she got her piercings.

"My mom went, against her dislike," Lassen said. "She's not really into anything like that."

But Lassen, who was paying for the piercings herself, said her mother went because she wanted to ensure that Lassen was getting pierced safely.

"She wanted to make sure everything was sterile," she said.

Meghan Bard, "Despite Parents' Concern, Body Piercings Stay Popular Among Teens," *Sentinel and Enterprise*, August 28, 2005. Reproduced by permission.

Parents Are More Accepting

Lassen's mother's quandary seems to be the norm, as more parents accept the reality that their kids want piercings.

Some parents are giving their consent to teen piercing because they fear their underage kids might try to do it themselves.

Christopher Kyprianos, the owner of BOD-MOD, USA in Gardner, [Massachusetts,] said about 50 percent of his piercing business is from teenagers under 18 who come in with their parents.

"The bellybutton is the most popular piercing," Kyprianos said. "A lot of the girls are looking to do that when they're 15, 16 years old."

Piercings and tattoos are definitely in the mainstream right now. They'll never go down. It won't be a fad that just fades out.

Andy Von, 23, of Shirley, [Massachusetts,] said his parents took him to get his first piercings when he was 15 or 16. Von no longer has a labret piercing, which is a piercing just below the lip, or his septum pierced, which is a piercing through the cartilage between the nostrils.

Piercings Are Less Permanent

Von, who also works as a tattoo artist, said piercings are a less-permanent form of being different and rebellious.

"You see a lot of younger kids getting (piercings)," Von said. "It's a body modification, but they can take it out if they don't like it, unlike a tattoo."

Von said parents are more likely to go along with a piercing because it's not as bad as a tattoo.

"It's not such a big deal," he said. "(Piercings are) more mainstream, it's more accepted."

Andy Sansone, who works as a piercer at Evolution Body Art in Leominster, [Massachusetts] agreed with Von.

"Piercing and tattoos are definitely in the mainstream right now," he said. "They'll never go down. It won't be a fad that just fades out."

Sansone said Leominster is one of the few communities in the state that does not allow teens under 18 to get a body piercing, even with parental consent. The Board of Health in Leominster is considering changing the regulations to allow minors to get piercings with a parent's consent.

"I've had angry mothers come in and yell at me," Sansone said. "The parents obviously want to bring them into the shop."

And with good reason.

Life-threatening Complications

A 13-year-old girl Boston girl almost died this month [August 2005] after her mother, Deborah Robinson, failed to take her to a doctor for weeks after the girl tried to pierce her own navel and a life-threatening infection occurred.

"It can be very dangerous," Sansone said of self piercing. "If you have a jagged or improper tool it can tear the tissue and be more susceptible to infection."

Kyprianos said teens aren't aware of the fact that alcohol isn't a sterilizer, and that they could be exposing themselves to HIV, hepatitis or tuberculosis.

"They're not wearing gloves. They're not using sterilized jewelry and equipment," Kyprianos said of self-piercers. "They have no knowledge of anatomy. They have no knowledge of after-care (procedures)."

Aftercare

Kyprianos said if people properly follow the after-care procedures that he gives them verbally and in writing, they will rarely have a problem with their piercing.

But he does encourage customers to come back with any concerns about their piercing.

"If something doesn't feel right or look right, pick up the phone and call us or stop in the store," Kyprianos said.

Sisters Abby, 16, and Winnie Clark, 13, of Petersham, [Massachusetts,] were shopping together at the mall at Whitney Field.

Abby Clark got her eyebrow pierced, and she plans to get her nose pierced in the next couple of months. She said she likes the decoration piercings give her face.

"I just like the sparkle," she said. "I like the little jewels."

Abby Clark's mother went with her to get the piercing, but her father, a chemistry teacher, is totally against them.

"He's all body conservative," she said.

Little sister Winnie Clark said she wants to follow in her sister's footsteps, and get a couple piercings of her own, in her nose and an industrial piercing in her ear—two piercings through the cartilage of the ear are joined together with one barbell.

She hopes to be able to get the piercings by the time she's 15.

"It wouldn't be fair to Abby if I got it earlier than she did," Winnie Clark said.

But big sister issued a note of caution.

"It takes a lot of convincing," Abby Clark said with a laugh.

10

Employers Are Becoming More Accepting of Body Art

Mielikki Org

Mielikki Org is a staff reporter for the Wall Street Journal.

Due to the increasing popularity of tattoos and body piercings among Soccer Moms and white-collar workers, corporate America is becoming more accepting of body art on its employees. Many businesses will permit their employees to sport tattoos or body piercings as long as they are not offensive or do not endanger their workers. Some employee tattoos or body piercing may even enhance a company's image.

Tattoos started their migration from the biceps of sailors to celebrity bellybuttons and collegiate female midriffs about a decade ago without much of an uproar. Now they are finding acceptance in a more unlikely environment: the workplace.

Moving Into the Mainstream

Ford Motor Co. allows employees from the most senior executives on down to have tattoos and piercings, except those that could endanger factory workers. The same goes for Boeing Co. In Silicon Valley, the tech industry law firm Wilson, Sonsini, Goodrich, & Rosati counts a few tattooed and pierced attorneys among its staff. Vincent Weiner, a tattoo artist in Los

Angeles, says everyone from federal judges to a retired corporate vice president is lining up for body art these days.

"It's no longer a subculture urge," says Mr. Weiner, who worked as director of operations for a San Francisco hedge-fund company, before deciding to move to Los Angeles to pursue tattoo artistry, his true love.

While more people in the office are turning up with tattoos and piercings, it's not always because of some sweeping change in corporate policy. Often, in fact, companies leave it up to individual managers to set the rules for the employees who report to them. And, while a number of executives are now getting body art, that doesn't mean it's always visible to their co-workers and clients.

But companies that are more accepting about body adornment say they are just going with the times, trying to take advantage of the open-mindedness and innovation that younger employees bring into the workplace. Such shifting attitudes have helped make tattooing one of the faster-growing retail businesses in the U.S. The word "tattoo" is one of the most popular search words on the Internet, according to the search engine Lycos, and tattoo artists from California to New York report that their earnings have doubled within the past decade.

Increasingly More Popular

In all, one in every 10 Americans have tattoos, up from one out of every hundred three decades ago, according to the Alliance of Professional Tattooists based in Annapolis, Md. Upper-middle-class women between the ages of 20 and 40, especially those that dread mutating later in life into Soccer Moms, fuel most of the growth, according to tattoo parlors.

Then there are people like Paul Hempel. He is 54 years old and the senior executive lawyer for Inverness Medical Innovations Inc., a medical-products company in Boston. Five years ago [in 1998] he got a tattoo, and now, a menagerie decorates his upper torso, including a phoenix, a dragon and an eagle. A lion and yin-yang symbol adorn his legs. And he wears a diamond stud in his left ear.

"People comment on them and say, 'Gosh, a corporate counsel with tattoos,' but not in a negative sense," says Mr. Hempel, whose body art attracts attention at company picnics. "Some people think it's kind of cool to have a senior executive of counsel who's a little bit on the edge." (Mr. Hempel's various tattoos aren't visible when he's wearing his business attire.)

No Longer Strictly Blue Collar

Tattoos used to be strictly a blue-collar domain, but the few big companies that have rules governing them tend to be service-oriented industries. Wal-Mart Stores Inc. forbids all facial piercings and asks employees to cover "offensive" tattoos—which it defines as any that are violent or profane. Subway Restaurants limits piercings to the ears, and even then, allows no more than one hole per ear. While U.S. postal carriers can freely display tattoos, cashiers at McDonald's cannot.

As wearers become more white-collar, the tattoos themselves—and the brightly lit studios that offer them—are becoming increasingly upscale and artistic as well. Patrons can opt for anything from Japanese Hokusai waves or Erte's slender, line-drawn females to memorials to Auschwitz and Sept. 11. Mr. Weiner, the Los Angeles tattoo artist, says people are looking for more "thoughtful" and "focused" pieces than when the tattoo craze hit eight years ago.

Mr. Hempel, the Inverness lawyer, says he "doesn't flaunt his tattoos around the office." According to a 2001 survey on tattoos in the workplace from the Internet site Vault.com, which deals with work issues, the most popular placements of tattoos are areas that can be hidden: the backs, arms and legs.

But according to Holly English, a consultant for the New Jersey-based firm Values at Work, which advises companies on values and ethics, a few ounces of permanent ink or a third earring hole can help employees retain a sense of dignity and independence when they don the yoke of the corporate workplace. "It's an interesting and very healthy way to project a little bit of personality without coming on so strong that it does damage to the office or client relationship," she says.

Body Art Can Help Business

And sometimes, these creative markings can even enhance a company's image. Although colleagues initially ribbed Christof Koch, a neuroscientist and California Institute of Technology professor, about the Macintosh Apple logo he got tattooed on his right shoulder three years ago, most approve. "[It] adds to the mystique of the 'crazy scientist,'" Mr. Koch said. Apple features Mr. Koch and his tattoo on its corporate Web site.

Scott Fenton, president of Lodestar Capital Group, where Mr. Weiner used to work, says his former employee's unusual appearance sometimes even helped business. That was especially true, he said, when he sent Mr. Weiner, who has tattoos covering his back and entire right arm, piercing on his lower lip, and one-inch wood-and-bone ear discs, to meet with staid bank representatives.

"Just because [the bank representative] isn't in his mode, he would actually hear what we're saying," Mr. Fenton said. "It's an unusual but effective way of doing business."

11

Employers May Regulate Body Art on Their Employees

Louis Pechman

Louis Pechman is a lawyer who specializes in labor and employment law.

Neither federal nor state law protects employees from discrimination due to their tattoos or body piercing. Fired employees have filed lawsuits against their employers claiming religious discrimination, sex discrimination, and a violation of free speech with little success. Several courts have found that as long as employers apply their dress codes standards uniformly, employers may dictate what body art their employees may and may not display.

It is generally recognized that employers are free to set reasonable dress codes and grooming standards that are business-justified and applied in a nondiscriminatory manner.

In the case of individuals with tattoos and piercings, there is no federal or state law that affords them explicit protection from employment discrimination on the basis of their appearance. Employees in such cases have met with limited success in trying to establish a connection between their body art and a protected class such as religion, gender or national origin.

Piercings

In *Cloutier v. Costco Wholesale*, Kimberly Cloutier, a Costco cashier who was terminated after refusing to remove her eyebrow piercing, alleged that she was discriminated against based

Louis Pechman, "Keeping Up Appearances at Work," *New York Law Journal*, December 16, 2005. Reproduced by permission.

on her religion. Cloutier refused to comply with Costco's dress code prohibiting facial or tongue jewelry, citing her membership in the Church of Body Modification, which practices piercing, tattooing, branding, transdermal or subcutaneous implants and body manipulation such as flesh hook suspensions and pulling. The church proclaims that it is aimed at achieving acceptance in society so that its members may "celebrate their bodies with modification." Cloutier rejected Costco's proposed accommodation to cover her eyebrow piercing with a flesh-colored bandage, insisting that she be exempted from the dress code because her religion required her to display her facial jewelry at all times.

A dress code policy is permissible under federal and state discrimination laws as long as it is enforced on an equal basis.

The 1st U.S. Circuit Court of Appeals found that Costco had no duty to agree to Cloutier's request that she be exempted from the dress code. In the court's view, such an accommodation would pose an undue hardship because it would have an adverse effect on Costco's legitimate business interest in maintaining a "neat, clean and professional image." The court held that a religious accommodation constitutes an undue hardship when it would impose upon an employer more than a de minimus cost, including lost business or noneconomic costs. The court recognized that "Costco is far from unique in adopting personal appearance standards to promote and protect its image" and observed that "courts have long recognized the importance of personal appearance regulations." Such dress codes, it added, which are designed to appeal to customer preference or promote a professional public image, have been upheld.

Dress Code Policies Are Legal

A dress code policy is permissible under federal and state discrimination laws as long as it is enforced on an equal basis. In *Kleinsorge v. Eyeland Corp.*, Frank Kleinsorge, an optometrist, was terminated "for cause" for wearing an earring to work in violation of a workplace rule prohibiting men from wearing jewelry. He sued, claiming that the company's policy was discriminatory because women were permitted to wear earrings while men were not. The U.S. District Court for the Eastern District of Pennsylvania dismissed the claim because Kleinsorge did not allege that the company's grooming policies were unevenly enforced as between male and female employees.

The Kleinsorge court relied heavily on a decision by the U.S. District Court for the Eastern District of New York, *Capaldo v. Pan American Federal Credit Union*, in which Judge Thomas C. Platt upheld a company policy prohibiting male employees from wearing earrings. Robert Capaldo, a loan counselor, was informed by the company's president that he did not present an appropriate professional image and was terminated for failing to remove his earring. The court, describing the company's policy as a "minor sex-based distinction in dress and grooming codes," dismissed the claim because there was no allegation that the company's policy was unevenly applied. Specifically, Capaldo did not assert that female employees at the company were free from all grooming standards or that the company unevenly applied its grooming policies as among male and female employees. Because the company did not impose special appearance rules on one sex and not the other, no inference of sex discrimination arose.

More recently, the Supreme Court of Iowa agreed that a company's grooming code that forbade male employees from wearing earrings at work did not constitute sex-based discrimination. In *Pecenka v. Fareway Stores, Inc.*, Michael Pecenka, a Fareway Stores employee was terminated for refusing to remove his ear stud while he worked. The court rejected Pecenka's claim of disparate treatment, noting that the discrimination laws "were not meant to prohibit employers from instituting personal grooming codes which have a de minimus affect on employment." Because the court concluded that the earring policy did not rise to the level of sex-based discrimination, the company did not need a business justification for it. The court also dismissed the claim of "sex-plus" discrimination, because wearing an earring is not an "immutable characteristic" and does not involve a "fundamental right" such as the right to marry or bear children and the company's earring policy was not alleged to perpetuate a sexist or chauvinistic attitude in employment that significantly affected employment opportunities.

Tattoos

The unequal application of employment policies is always a source of potential liability for employers. In *Hub Folding Box Company, Inc. v. Massachusetts Commission Against Discrimination*, Deborah Connor, a clerk at the Hub Folding Box Co., sued her employer for gender discrimination and retaliation. Although a male employee was not required to cover his Navy tattoo, Connor was told to cover a heart-shaped tattoo on her forearm or be terminated. The company was concerned that customers who saw Connor's tattoo would have a negative reaction because a tattoo on a woman "symbolized that she was either a prostitute, on drugs, or from a broken home." In the employer's view, women with tattoos were ne'er-do-wells, whereas men with tattoos were heroes. The employer's reasoning, according to the court, was based on outdated gender stereotypes and constituted an unlawful basis for treating men and women differently in the workplace.

Disparate treatment was also the basis of a discrimination claim in *Riggs v. City of Forth Worth*. Michael Riggs, a police officer, sued the Fort Worth, Texas, police department for discrimination because of his Celtic national origin, race and fundamental right of free expression. While other officers in the bike unit with tattoos were allowed to wear shorts and short sleeves, the department claimed that Riggs' tattoos were excessive to the point of being unprofessional. Riggs' tattoos included a Celtic tribal band, a Celtic design that included his wife's name, a mermaid, a family crest, the cartoon character Jessica Rabbit and a two-foot by two-foot full-color rendering on his back of St. Michael spearing Satan. The court found that Riggs failed to provide any evidence that the department's reasons for requiring him to wear long sleeves and pants or for transferring him out of his unit were discriminatory.

The Nature of the Images

The nature of the images depicted by tattoos weighs in the balance where claims of religious discrimination are made. In *Swartzentruber v. Gunite Corp.*, Sheldon Swartzentruber, a member of the Church of the American Knights of the Klu Klux Klan, sued his employer for religious discrimination after being terminated because of his tattoo, which extended from his elbow to his wrist, depicting a hooded figure standing in front of a burning cross. The court held that the company reasonably accommodated Swartzentruber's asserted religious beliefs by allowing him to continue working so long as he covered his tattoo. Any alternative accommodation, the court suggested, would have imposed an undue hardship on both the company and Swartzentruber because the tattoo offended his coworkers and made them uncomfortable. Moreover, the court held that a claim for hostile environment harassment could not succeed because any harassment was a result of self-identification as a Klu Klux Klan member, not because of religious beliefs.

Constitutional Issues

Prohibitions against tattoos in the workplace have also been challenged on First Amendment grounds. Courts that have considered the issue have found that tattoos are not protected speech under the First Amendment. For example, the 8th U.S. Circuit Court of Appeals concluded that, "the tattoo is nothing more than 'self expression,' unlike other forms of expression or conduct which receive First Amendment protection." Because tattoos are not protected expression, an employer must show merely that the challenged classification is rationally related to a legitimate state interest rather than having to meet the more stringent strict scrutiny standard.

Even when a tattoo is deemed speech on a matter of public concern, the public interest at issue has been found to outweigh the employee's interest in displaying their tattoo. For example, in *Baldetta v. Harborview Medical Center*, John Baldetta, an HIV-positive hospital employee, was terminated after refusing to cover a tattoo saying "HIV positive." In finding that the hospital's interest in facilitating patients' recovery outweighed Baldetta's interest in "speaking" on a matter of public concern, the court relied on the opinion of doctors who concluded that display of the tattoo could cause stress in patients and hinder their recovery.

Employees have also failed to establish that the right to display tattoos is protected by the First Amendment right to free association and privacy. In *Montoya v. Giusto*, a group of corrections deputies alleged that their First Amendment rights were violated after they were terminated for displaying tattoos that read "Brotherhood of Strong." The U.S. District Court for the District of Oregon found that the decision to wear the tattoos did not enjoy constitutional protection because the tattoos, which signified "a loosely knit friendship of weight lifters," was not the kind of political, social, economic, educational, religious or cultural association protected by the First Amendment.

Statutory Protections

A few local jurisdictions have enacted legislation prohibiting discrimination on the basis of appearance. The District of Columbia has prohibited discrimination on the basis of "personal appearance." Similarly, the city of Santa Cruz, Calif., has a statute barring discrimination on the basis of "physical characteristics." A unique statute in Madison, Wis., classifies "physical appearance" as a protected class, defining it in terms of immutable characteristics, such as height, weight and facial features, but also includes mutable characteristics like hairstyle, beards and manner of dress.

Tattoos and piercings are voluntary body art that an employer may choose to exclude from the workplace.

Although Wisconsin's statute protects appearance, employer requirements that are uniformly applied "in a business establishment for a reasonable business purpose" are exempted. The breadth of protection afforded by this statute was tested in *Sam's Club Inc. v. Madison Equal Opportunities Comm'n*, which the Madison Equal Opportunities Commission decided that Sam's Club had violated the ordinance by terminating an employee who wore an eyebrow ring in violation of company dress code. The Wisconsin Court of Appeals reversed, stating "Sam's Club attempts to project . . . a conservative, no frills, no flash image for its business; it does so because Sam's Club wants to convey to customers that they are getting the best value for their money." The court noted it was undisputed that facial jewelry and eyebrow rings in particular do not convey a conservative image. Inasmuch as Sam's Club's prohibition came within that exception of a "reasonable business purpose," its decision to terminate was held to be legal.

In sum, individuals with piercings or tattoos have limited rights in the workplace. It is the rare case where a protected characteristic of an employee is so inextricably linked with a piercing or tattoo that it implicates legal interest. Underlying this lack of protection is that tattoos and piercings are neither explicitly protected by statute nor immutable characteristics.

Rather, tattoos and piercings are voluntary body art that an employer may choose to exclude from the workplace.

12

Some Religions Embrace Body Modification

Austin Cline

Austin Cline is a regional director for the Council for Secular Humanism and a former publicity coordinator for the Campus Freethought Alliance.

A woman fired by a hospital for wearing a lip ring claims that her piercings comprise an important part of her religion. Simply because the Church of Body Modification is not a mainstream religion does not make its beliefs any less valid. The government must either develop a clear definition for what constitutes a "religion" or else extend its religious exemptions to all religions, regardless of how mainstream America views such beliefs.

How narrowly can government or employers define "religion" when it comes to protecting people from discrimination against what they say is religious behavior? That's a difficult question and the boundaries of the answer are being tested in Albany, New York, where Sarah Yule was fired from St. Mary's Hospital for refusing to remove her lip ring which she says she wears for religious reasons.

The Chuch of Body Modification

The [Albany] *Times Union* reports:

> Yule's religion has no formal deity or buildings of worship. Some of its adherents suspend themselves by hooks dug into their skin. You can apply to be a minister by e-mail.

Austin Cline, "Church of Body Modification Complains About Religious Discrimination," About.com: Agnosticism/Atheism, August 25, 2006. Reproduced by permission.

Yule, 24, of Waterford, says she is a member of the Church of Body Modification, whose members meet online to share a passion for changing their bodies.

There has been at least one previous suit brought by a member of the Church of Body Modification against an employer they accused of religious discrimination but they lost. According to the Massachusetts court in that case, it would have imposed an "undue hardship" on Costco to allow a person to continue openly wearing an eyebrow ring. However, the court never ruled on whether the Church of Body Modification is a "real" religion so there is still room for a different decision. Unfortunately, Yule hasn't even been able to find a lawyer to take her case yet.

"This wouldn't be an issue if I were a Catholic or a Jew or a well-known religion," she said less than 12 hours after she was fired from her job as a receptionist in the hospital's emergency room, where she had worked for two years.

Traditional Religions Versus Minority Religions

She's right. Members of traditional and larger religions have a much easier time getting exemptions to neutral laws and regulations than members of minority groups. I think that one reason is the fact that these aren't so much "exemptions" as they are special privileges: religious believers see "exemptions" as the best way to maintain their access to special privileges in a secular society but being privileged doesn't mean much if those privileges are open to any Johnny Come Lately who claims to have a new religion. So they insist on defining "religion" as narrowly as possible so as to include only as many religious groups as absolutely necessary. Keeping the club exclusive ensures that the value of the privileges is maintained.

Is there any validity to calling her piercings are part of her religion? She claims that they are spiritual because they give her control over her body. Perhaps that sounds odd, but how is that any more odd than the Muslim belief that women should have their hair covered? Not very, likely.

If there were health and safety considerations, then the hospital has a stronger case even if the Church of Body Modification is a "real" religion and even if the piercings are legitimate religious behavior. After all, a person's right to engage in religious behavior cannot extend to the point where others are put in danger and hospitals have an especially strong obligation to protect the health and safety of people who come to them. However, Yule isn't a nurse and doesn't work directly with patients in a way that should cause people to be very concerned.

Body modifications play an important role in religions and cultures all over—and have done so for millennia.

Yule's job was as a receptionist and in such a position her body modifications should have been irrelevant. According to the letter she received from the hospital's human resources department, she needed to remove the lip ring "to maintain a professional environment." So, safety and health aren't at issue here.

> The question is whether body piercings are a protected form of religious observance, whether a tongue ring should be given the same protection as a Muslim head scarf under the law. "It's very sticky," said Stephen Clark, a professor at Albany Law School who specializes in employment, labor and constitutional law. "It's extremely difficult to pin this thing down, what religion means."

No Clear Definition of Religion

Stephen Clark is right that it's difficult to create a clear definition of religion. Unfortunately, so long as the government insists on giving special privileges to people on the basis of "religion," the government is obligated to create such a definition—and, moreover, ensure that it's a fair definition which covers all religions, not just traditional and larger religions. This will annoy the people who want to keep the list of those with access to religious "exemptions" as short as possible, but it's something they are bringing on themselves by constantly pushing to get more and more of these "exemptions" for their lives.

> The [Church of Body Modification] describes itself as "a nondenominational congregation that teaches ownership over our own bodies . . . not here to offer spirituality to you so much as we are here because of the spirituality that is already in all of us." It was established in 1999. . . . The church Web site addresses questions about employment and tells people that "this is not a scam" and that they cannot join after they've been fired just to protect their jobs.

All of this sounds completely fair. I'll admit that I find the idea of a "Church of Body Modification" to be very odd, but at the same time I'm familiar with enough world religions to know that body modifications play an important role in religions and cultures all over—and have done so for millennia. Modifying the body in the context of religious beliefs is nothing new and so while it may be odd to have a church defined by that, it's really not at all odd for someone to say that modifying their body is part of their religious practice.

There's a lot more continuity between this Church of Body Modification and traditional religious beliefs than there is between the Raelians and traditional religions. So if the Raelians can be declared a religion under the law, then this church shouldn't even be given a second thought before it's approved.

13

Some Religions Forbid Tattoos

Awake!

Awake! *is a monthly magazine published by Jehovah's Witnesses.*

Getting a tattoo may give some youths a feeling of power and control over their lives, but the Old Testament forbade tattoos. While today's Christians are not bound by Old Testament law, tattoos—even temporary ones—suggest paganism and idol worship. Many people react negatively to those with tattoos, which could lead to problems when it is time to find a job or pursue personal relationships. Many people come to regret having a tattoo. It is best not to get one in the first place.

Tattoos are everywhere—so it seems. Rock stars, sports figures, fashion models, and movie stars flaunt them. Many teenagers have followed suit, proudly displaying tattoos on their shoulders, hands, waists, and ankles. Andrew contends: "Tattoos are cool. Having one or not is a personal choice."

Says the *World Book Encyclopedia*: "Tattooing is the practice of making permanent designs on the body. It is done by pricking small holes in the skin with a sharpened stick, bone, or needle that has been dipped in pigments with natural colors."

Although exact statistics are hard to come by, one source estimates that 25 percent of all 15- to 25-year-olds in the United States have a tattoo. Sandy says: "It's the popular thing to do." Why are tattoos so appealing to some youths?

Awake!, "Young People Ask ... Should I Get a Tattoo?" www.watchtower.org, September 22, 2003. Copyright © Watch Tower Bible and Tract Society of Pennsylvania. Reproduced by permission.

Why So Popular?

For some, a tattoo is a way of making a grand romantic gesture. Michelle relates: "On his ankle my brother has the name of a girl he used to go out with." The problem? "He's not dating her anymore." According to *Teen* magazine, "Doctors estimate that more than 30 percent of all tattoo removal is done on teen girls who want the name of an ex-boyfriend taken off."

Some youths view tattoos as works of art. Others see them as symbols of independence. "I'm in charge of my life," proclaimed Josie, adding that getting a tattoo was "the only life decision I've ever made." Tattooing allows some youths to experiment—to feel they have control over their appearance. Tattoos can also serve as a symbol of rebellion or of alternative lifestyles. Some tattoos thus contain obscene words and drawings or provocative slogans.

The Mosaic Law forbade God's people to tattoo themselves.

The majority of youths, however, may simply have become caught up in a fad. But just because it seems as if everyone is getting tattooed, does it mean that *you* should?

The Ancient Art of Tattooing

Tattooing is by no means a modern practice. Tattoo-bearing Egyptian and Libyan mummies have been found that date back hundreds of years before the time of Christ. Tattooed mummies have also been found in South America. Many of the tattooed images were directly related to the worship of pagan gods. According to researcher Steve Gilbert, "the earliest known tattoo that is a picture of something, rather than an abstract pattern, represents the god Bes. In Egyptian mythology Bes is the lascivious god of revelry."

Significantly, the Mosaic Law forbade God's people to tattoo themselves. Said *Leviticus 19:28*: "You must not make cuts in your flesh for a deceased soul, and you must not put tattoo marking upon yourselves. I am Jehovah." Pagan worshipers, such as the Egyptians, tattooed the names or symbols of their deities on their breast or arms. By complying with Jehovah's ban on tattoo markings, the Israelites would stand out as different from other nations.—*Deuteronomy* 14:1, 2.

While Christians today are not under the Law of Moses, the prohibition it laid on tattooing is sobering (*Ephesians* 2:15; *Colossians* 2:14, 15). If you are a Christian, you would certainly not want to make markings on your body—even temporarily—that smack of paganism or false worship.—*2 Corinthians* 6:15–18.

Health Risks

There are also health concerns you should consider. Dr. Robert Tomsick, an associate professor of dermatology, comments: "What you're doing is breaking the skin and introducing pigmented material into the area. Even though the needle only goes in a little way, anytime you break the skin, you have a risk of bacterial or viral infection. I think [getting a tattoo] is generally a risky thing to do." Dr. Tomsick continues: "Once pigment is in, even if there's no infection, there's always the chance of contact allergies, dermatitis and allergic reactions that can cause skin to get red, swollen, crusty and itchy."

You should also give serious thought to how others might feel about your wearing a tattoo.

Despite the intended permanence of tattoos, various methods are used in attempts to remove them: Laser removal (burning the tattoo away), surgical removal (cutting the tattoo away), dermabrasion (sanding the skin with a wire brush to remove the epidermis and dermis), salabrasion (using a salt solution to soak the tattooed skin), and scarification (removing the tattoo with an acid solution and creating a scar in its place). These methods are expensive and can be painful. "It's more painful to have a tattoo removed by laser than to get the original tattoo," says *Teen* magazine.

What Will Others Think?

You should also give serious thought to how others might feel about your wearing a tattoo, as many react negatively (*1 Corinthians* 10:29–33). On a whim, Li, a woman in Taiwan, got a tattoo at age 16. Now she is a 21-year-old office worker. "It bothers me the way my co-workers stare at the tattoo," Li admits. British mental-health worker Theodore Dalrymple says that to many people, tattoos "are often the visible sign that a man ... belongs to a violent, brutal, antisocial, and criminalized subculture."

An article in *American Demographics* magazine similarly observed: "It is clear that most Americans consider it risky to have visible body art. Eighty-five percent [of youths] agree with the statement, 'people who have visible tattoos ... should realize that this form of self-expression is likely to create obstacles in their career or personal relationships.'"

Consider also whether choosing to get a tattoo would enhance or undermine your claim of being a Christian. Could it be a "cause for stumbling" others? (*2 Corinthians* 6:3) True, some youths have had their tattoos placed on hidden areas of the body. Even their parents may not know about these secret tattoos. But beware! An emergency trip to the doctor or simply taking a shower at school could make your secret common knowledge! Better it is to "conduct ourselves honestly in all things," avoiding foolish deception.—Hebrews 13:18.

Like all fads, tattoos may lose their appeal over time. Really, is there any garment—whether a pair of jeans, a shirt, a dress, or a pair of shoes—that you love so much that you would commit to wearing it for the rest of your life? Of course not! Styles, cuts, and colors change. Unlike a piece of clothing, however, tattoos are hard to shed. Besides, what is "cool" to you when you are 16 might not be very appealing when you are 30.

Many have come to regret making permanent alterations to their appearance. "I got a tattoo before learning about Jehovah," relates Amy. "I try to keep it covered. When others in the congregation happen to see it, I feel embarrassed." The message? Think before you ink. Don't make a decision that you may regret later.

14

Most People Love
Their Tattoos

Kristopher Kaiyala

Kristopher Kaiyala is a writer based in Washington State.

Body art is no longer reserved for social outcasts such as bikers, criminals, and sailors. Tattoos are becoming increasingly common on Americans of all ages and are considered by many to be "art," not skin graffiti. Perceptions about tattoos are changing, and body art is becoming more acceptable, even by senior citizens.

It was a typical family vacation in Honolulu. Kathryn visited many of the usual attractions: Waikiki Beach, Pearl Harbor, Diamond Head . . . and a tattoo shop. On a lark while sightseeing, she and her two female companions walked in.

They each walked out with small designs—in Kathryn's case, a rose, to symbolize her hometown of Portland, Ore.—permanently imprinted on their right ankles, discreetly placed to not draw attention, but to easily show off to friends without making them blush.

Many would argue there are better ways to immortalize a vacation than getting a tattoo, but stories like Kathryn's are becoming more and more common. Today, it seems people of every persuasion are doing it. Case in point: At the time of her vacation, Kathryn was 75.

"When I got back home," she says with a laugh, "everybody at my retirement complex thought it was absolutely fantastic! Except for one person; she thought it was just horrible."

Kristopher Kaiyala, "The Skin Game: Once 'Graffitti,' Now Body Art," MSNBC.com, 2007. Republished with permission of MSNBC.com.

So the next time you talk to grandma on the phone, ask her if she's been to the parlor lately—the *tattoo* parlor.

Going Mainstream?

Body art is no longer the domain of bikers, sailors and inmates. A 2003 online survey by Harris Interactive found that 16 percent of all U.S. adults have at least one tattoo. The age group with the highest number of tattooed adults is 25–29 year-olds (36 percent), followed by 30–39 year olds (28 percent). Seven percent of tattoo owners are 65 and older. The poll also found that equal numbers of males and females have received tattoos.

If you think tattoos are a recent phenomenon, needle this: Many unearthed Egyptian mummies have shown evidence of body art, and it's likely that the practice originated much earlier. The word "tattoo" entered the English vernacular some time around 1785, when Captain Cook observed in his journal that Tahitians engaged in the art of *tattau* ("to mark").

For various reasons over the years, tattoos became taboo in Western cultures—but this is rapidly changing. From Dennis Rodman to David Beckham, from the Dixie Chicks to Cher, from 50 Cent to Eminem, athletes, celebrities and others in the media have brought tattoos into the limelight. Today tattoos are considered by aficionados as "art," not skin graffiti.

Coming of Age

If tattoos are becoming more mainstream, the tattoo industry is growing up as well. There now exists a National Tattoo Association (with annual conventions), as well as an Alliance of Professional Tattooists (APT), whose primary mission is to educate shop owners on critical health and safety issues.

No one knows for certain how many adults had tattoos 10 or even 20 years ago, but Dennis Dwyer, a director at the Tucson, Ariz.-based APT, says the industry has grown sharply in the last decade. Today his organization has around 3,000 members. Five years ago, it was around 1,800.

"We're still seeing more and more people getting tattoos," notes Dwyer, "but interestingly, the industry is reaching a saturation point; there are so many shops out there now that it may not be as lucrative for the average tattooist as it once was." Dwyer also notes that a lot of business is being lost to so-called underground tattooists—amateur "artists" who tattoo friends and family members for free or for cash on the side with little regard for industry standards.

"People come in for a tattoo, they like what they get and how they're treated, and come back for more."

But not all shops are in a rut. According to the Harris poll, the Western United States has more tattooed adults than any other region in the country. And that makes sense to shop owner Karen Roze of Sacred Rose Tattoo in San Francisco's Mission District. These days, she says, business is booming.

Parlor Gone Boutique?

Ask anyone to describe a typical tattoo shop and you may hear words like "seedy," "dirty," "macho." Roze, 37, is out to change that perception by mixing her art with friendliness and customer service. In San Francisco, a hotbed of tattoo artists and tattoo seekers, competition can be fierce.

"We train our artists to treat each customer as if their tattoo was the most important thing to them," says Roze, who opened her shop in 1998 after apprenticing for about six years elsewhere. Roze shies away from any salon-type comparisons, but she insists her shop's open layout (no booths) and clean, old-fashioned atmosphere create a very professional and creative environment.

You'd expect nothing less from a fine-arts graduate. In fact, each artist in Roze's shop is schooled in the arts. Roze says the high-quality designs they come up with draw clients in the door more than once. "People come in for a tattoo, they like what they get and how they're treated, and come back for more. I'm even tattooing children of parents that I tattooed years earlier."

What surprises Roze most in recent years is how many of her clients are senior citizens. "I have a theory," she says, "that the older you get, the less you care about what others think. Plus you have more disposable income. A good tattoo isn't cheap."

The Harris poll revealed another telling statistic: 34 percent of tattooed adults feel sexier than before getting their body art. Roze concurs. "The fake tattoos were always the coolest prize in the Cracker Jack box. Now people don't have to worry about getting the real thing. The sexy appeal of body art never goes away."

15

Many People Regret Getting a Tattoo

Deanna Anderson

Deanna Anderson is a freelance writer.

Approximately one-third of people with a tattoo regret getting it. The most common reasons for regretting a tattoo is the tattoo is the name of a significant other who is no longer significant; it is a gang or prison tattoo; the tattoo is of poor quality; or the wearer regrets the location of the tattoo. Tattoos should never be done on a whim or a dare.

In a national survey in which 163 tattooed men and women were asked about their tattoos one-third of those men and women said they regretted their tattoo.

People Change As They Grow Older

The reasons for why someone regrets getting their tattoo vary as much as the reasons why they want to get them. People's likes, dislikes and affiliations change as they grow older and what someone likes or thinks is cool at age 20 will not be the same at age 50. For this reason, tattoos should never be done on a whim or to please someone else. It is permanent and the tattoo wearer has to live with it. Tattoos should also never be done while the wearer is drunk or intoxicated in any way; in fact, it is illegal to do so.

Choosing a tattoo should be a very personal and meaningful experience. There are two basic types of tattoos: flash and

Deanna Anderson, "Tattoo Designs You'll Regret," *Happy Living*, 2005. Reproduced by permission.

custom. A flash tattoo is the designs you see in stock at the tattoo parlor while a custom tattoo is one a customer brings in themselves. Either way, the decision should not be taken lightly. An aspiring tattoo wearer should choose a design that represents them.

Because of the permanency of your tattoo a person should look at themselves in 5, 10, or even 20 years. As a free-spirited college student a web of vines on the wrist would look really lovely. However, if that same student is planning on working in a very conservative field after graduation will others look at the tattoo negatively? If so, the tattoo wearer needs to decide if they can or are willing to cover up the tattoo either by cosmetics or clothing.

It is very expensive to remove a tattoo. Expect to pay $1,000 to remove even a fairly small-sized tattoo if you're looking at laser surgery. Also expect to have a noticeable ugly scar with a non-laser technique. Health insurance companies will not pay for tattoo removal because it is considered an aesthetic and elective surgery and not required for their physical health.

Common Reasons to Regret A Tattoo

Here are some common reasons why a tattoo might be regretted:

Lover's name. When in the throes of passion an aspiring tattoo wearer may decide to get the name of their significant other tattooed somewhere on their body. The only problem with this endearing symbolism is that when the significant other is not so significant anymore, the tattoo wearer is stuck with the name. Either a tattoo artist will have to be creative and cover up the tattoo or it will have to be removed.

Gang symbols. Often gang members will have special tattoos that will show status or involvement in a gang. While this may give a tattoo wearer special privileges within the gang it may subject them to the scrutiny of outsiders or make them a victim of other gangs simply because of the affiliation. A person who wants to leave a gang or put that past behind them will have a constant reminder of that time.

Prison tats. Like gang tattoos, prison tattoos have a symbolism and culture that is unique. Often prisoners tell their story by the tattoos placed on their body. These tattoos can identify what the prisoner is in for, what they are willing to do, if they can be trusted or not and many other things. And, like the gang tattoos these representations can be reminders to the wearer or cause them to be under the scrutiny of others.

Location. The location of a tattoo should not be taken lightly. Depending on a person's career choice a visible tattoo might just hinder their gaining a position in that field or career. Many places from fast food chains on up to administrative positions will not hire a person with a visible tattoo. If it can be covered up, for example on the ankle or shoulder, it is allowed. Facial tattoos are not highly recommended because they cannot be covered up and to be removed by laser surgery is risky and may leave scarring. Also, an ill-placed tattoo may leave a customer feeling less than satisfied. A tattoo that is crooked or askew on a part of the body, or not centered on the body part will not likely be valued much.

Other Reasons

Cartoons, musicians, actors. Tattooing a favorite cartoon character, actor or band is often done as a symbolic gesture to honor that thing. However, as a person grows older their likes may change. A person might suddenly be 50 years old and will be stuck with a cartoon tattooed on their arm. Or the musicians and actors they liked at one time might not be so important anymore. There is also the added concern over copyright and trademark infringement as well. Some companies have tried to sue people and tattoo artists for duplicating their images.

Poor quality. Any tattoo that comes out in a poor quality is also one that will be regretted. Lines might be blurred, text might be misspelled, lines might be shaky, borders or details might not be uniform, colors might be faded or dull. Home-made or prison-made tattoos are more likely to have these problems but they can also be encountered in a tattoo parlor. Make sure you view a portfolio of the artist's work before and talk with the tattoo artist so you can get a feel for their work.

Whims or dares. As stated earlier, a tattoo should be a very personal decision and not one that is done on the spur of the moment or done as a dare or a favor to someone else. Getting a tattoo for someone else takes away the personal aspect of it and will likely be regretted later by the one who has to wear it.

16

Tattoos Are Part of Military Tradition

Finnbar McCallion

Finnbar McCallion was a soldier stationed at the Public Affairs Office at Fort Dix, New Jersey, at the time he wrote this article.

Tattoos have been a part of military history for thousands of years. American sailors were originally tattooed to record where they had sailed and as good luck talismans. Other services have also adopted tattoos as a way to commemorate their military experiences and as a form of personal identity.

Good tattoos aren't cheap and cheap tattoos aren't good.

Somewhere out there is a girl with a tattoo of a man's name on her derrière. She begs the question, "Who does that sort of thing?"

Members marked in ink include Queen Victoria, Alice Cooper, John F. Kennedy Jr., Sean Connery, and Winston Churchill's mother. A tattoo butterfly even graced the skin of a Barbie doll.

"I got my tattoos because I was allowed to get them; you better believe I asked my mother first," said Los Angeles Laker's Shaquille O'Neal in a *Rocky Mountain News* article.

Throughout history, tattoos have borne the mark of ill repute. But a sign of the times may be when biceps, bellies, ankles, forearms, butts and breasts fairly burst with their presence.

Finnbar McCallion, "Should Soldiers Choose Tattoos?" in *Ft. Dix, NJ Post Online*, March 26, 2004. Reproduced by permission.

This month [March 2004] saw the country's oldest continuously operating tattoo parlor stay afloat despite efforts of local homeowner groups to shut it down. Bert Grimm's World Famous Tattoo Shop in Long Beach, Calif. won its legal battles, and will continue to inject indelible ink into customers like it did back in 1927 when sailors from the Seventh Fleet pulled in.

Legal hassles or not, tattoos may soon be invading your neighborhood. According to *U.S. News & World Report*, tattooing is the country's sixth-fastest growing retail business. And it's growing at the startling rate of more than one new tattoo studio every day. Nationwide, Oklahoma and South Carolina are the only two states where tattooing is still illegal. But regardless of the law, clandestine tattoo shops still thrive. [Both states have legalized tattoo parlors since this article was written.]

So how did the notorious art form ever rise to such popularity?

The world's first illustrated man wasn't Bradbury's and didn't crawl out from primordial ooze, either. It is universally believed that tattooed skin first made its mark on humanity in Egypt 5,000 years ago. However, after the discovery of the tattooed Ice Man in 1991, speculation traces tattoos' origins back even further to the dawn of mankind.

Tattoos and the Military

And tattoos appeared in military warfare earlier than one could imagine.

The last time tattooing reached such a height of popularity in America was in the early 1900s. After World War I there was, however, a gradual decline until its use literally spiraled into an underworld associated with convicts and miscreants.

According to the National Maritime Museum, the tattoo never fell out of favor with the American sailor; members of the Navy adopting it as a rite of passage. In 1900 an estimated

90 percent of sailors in the United States Navy were tattooed. And in 1909, the government outlawed the recruitment of would-be sailors bearing indecent or obscene tattoos.

The Meanings of Tattoos in the Armed Forces

Sailors with a tattoo of an anchor proved that they had sailed the Atlantic Ocean. A full-rigged ship meant he shipped around Cape Horn. A Shellback Turtle indicated the sailor crossed the equator, and a dragon meant he served on a station in or near China. "Hold" tattooed on the knuckles of one hand and "fast" on the other were said to allow the bearer to grip the rigging better. Tattoos of a pig on one foot and a rooster on the other were said to protect a seaman from drowning. It was thought since both creatures avoid the water at any chance they would help get the sailor swiftly to shore if he fell overboard.

"I thought having tattoos was a mark of who you were and what you did," said John Ulrich, a retired Navy captain who, along with his wife, volunteers more than a 1,000 working hours a year on various issues ranging from the Army Emergency Relief to homeless veterans' concerns.

Sailors like Ulrich went to places like "Thieves Alley" in Yokosuka, Scollay Square in Boston and the Honolulu Tattoo district in Chinatown. One of Ulrich's tattoos was laid the old-fashioned way: A needle attached to a handle applies the tattoo by tapping it into your skin manually. Retirees may recall the popular tattoo artist, Painless Nail from Boston. One of Ulrich's tattoos was done by one of her apprentices.

"The popularity of tattoos among the armed forces was greatest in the Navy, with the Army second, and the Marines third. Far down the scale was the Air Force with only a numerical sprinkling," wrote Samuel M. Steward, Ph.D, in his book *Bad Boys and Tough Tattoos*.

"Nowadays teenage girls, pro basketball players . . . people who never did a minute in any service have tattoos. It's now a fashion statement," said Ulrich.

Americans with Tattoos

Eighty-three percent of Americans with tattoos do not regret getting them. Sixteen percent do. Of those 16 percent, two percent say they regret getting them because having them affects their job in some way. But the number one reason cited for feelings of regret about getting a tattoo was "because of a person's name in the tattoo," according to a survey conducted by Harris Interactive online during July 2003 among a nationwide sample of 2,215 adults.

The same poll found that 16 percent of all adults have at least one tattoo. Thirty-six percent of Americans age 25 to 29 have tattoos; the number drops to 28 percent for the 30 to 39 age group, and continues to drop in multiples of seven to age 64 with only 7 percent. Democrats are more likely to have tattoos than Republicans with rates of 18 percent and 14 percent, respectively. Surprisingly, the percentage of males versus females with tattoos is about equal.

From pagans to cannibals, onto bikers, criminals, service members, social outcasts and heavy-metal rockers, tattoos have steered a course straight toward normalcy, rising up from then-disreputable pool halls and prisons to the soccer moms of today.

"Lawyers, doctors and TV anchorman are getting tattoos, so it's not just bikers anymore; we have grandma coming in getting tattoos. It's true. I'm serious," said Staff Sgt. Vincent Velez Jr., a vehicle operator with the 1079th Installation Support Battalion. An artist in civilian life, Velez also owns and operates Philadelphia's Poison Apple Tattoo and Piercing Studio along with an airbrush shop down the block.

Tattoos and Secret Clearances

If you're worried about job opportunity in the service, secret clearance, perhaps you should consider talking to a recruiter.

In a military dominated by esprit de corps, is it difficult to understand a passion or desire to mark or record the time spent in service?

"Tattoos have become more common in this generation— but it doesn't prohibit applicants looking for a job from the military. Only the ASVAB [Armed Services Vocational Aptitude Battery test] score, a physical and their upstanding moral background determine jobs. The military doesn't disqualify people from jobs because of tattoos," said Sgt. 1st Class Eduardo Huertas, reserve recruiter, in the Army's Central New Jersey Recruiting Command out of Red Bank.

Military Tattoo Policies

Army Regulation 670-1, paragraph 1-8d covers the Army's policy on tattoos. The policy is that tattoos in plain sight on the neck, face, or head are prohibited. The policy focuses chiefly on tattoos that are racist, sexist, or extremist.

"The current policy right now as it stands regarding tattoos, is if you're wearing the long sleeve shirt from the Class A uniform the tattoo cannot be lower than the wrist bone for males; for females, the rule of thumb is, if they are wearing the Class A uniform skirt a tattoo cannot be oversized. It can't deter or detract, meaning when they put the stocking on it can't be loud," said Huertas.

Other military services have policies that don't vary widely from the Army's.

In an age of individuality, is it really hard to discern what's behind the popularity of tattoos? In a military dominated by espirit de corps, is it difficult to understand a passion or desire to mark or record the time spent in service?

Tattoos quench the need to stake out identity and to record places and experiences to memory. They're like diamonds. They last forever. And they never go away.

Organizations to Contact

The editors have compiled the following list of organizations concerned with the issues debated in this book. The descriptions are derived from materials provided by the organizations. All have publications or information available for interested readers. The list was compiled on the date of publication of the present volume; the information provided here may change. Be aware that many organizations take several weeks or longer to respond to inquiries, so allow as much time as possible.

Alliance of Professional Tattooists (APT)
9210 S. Highway 17-92, Maitland, FL 32751
(407) 831-5549
Web site: www.safe-tattoos.com

The alliance is an educational organization of professional tattooists who have joined together to address the health and safety issues facing the tattoo industry. Through education, knowledge, and activism, APT and its members promote the understanding that professional tattooing is a safe expression of art. Its Web site includes answers to frequently asked questions concerning the health and safety risks of tattooing.

American Society for Dermatologic Surgery (ASDS)
5500 Meadowbrook Dr., Suite 120
Rolling Meadows, IL 60008
(947) 956-0900 • fax: (947) 956-0999
e-mail: info@asds.net
Web site: www.asds.net

Dermatologic surgery includes cosmetic and medically necessary skin surgery and laser surgery to repair or improve the condition of the skin. The association maintains on its Web site the fact sheets "Tattoo Removal" and "Tips to Consider when Obtaining a Tattoo or Piercing."

Association of Professional Piercers (APP)

P.O. Box 1287, Lawrence, KS   66044
e-mail: info@safepiercing.org
Web site: www.safepiercing.org

The APP is an international non-profit association dedicated to the dissemination of vital health and safety information related to body piercing, piercers, health care providers and the general public. It publishes the quarterly journal *The Point* and its Web site contains answers to frequently asked questions about body piercing, piercing care, troubleshooting, and how to choose a piercer.

Centers for Disease Control and Prevention (CDC)

1600 Clifton Rd., Atlanta, GA   30333
(404) 639-3534
e-mail: inquiry@cdc.gov
Web site: www.cdc.gov

The CDC is the government agency charged with protecting the public health of the nation by preventing and controlling diseases and by responding to public health emergencies. People who receive tattoos or body piercing are at risk of contracting blood-borne diseases such as hepatitis and HIV through dirty needles. Among the fact sheets on the CDC's Web site about the health risks associated with body modification is one titled "Can I get HIV from getting a tattoo or through body piercing?"

Food and Drug Administration (FDA)

5600 Fishers Lane, Rockville, MD   20857-0001
(888) 463-6332
Web site: www.fda.gov

The FDA is responsible for creating and enforcing regulations for cosmetic safety. Cosmetic products and ingredients are not subject to FDA premarket approval authority, with the exception of color additives. The pigments used in tattoo inks are considered additives and as such are subject to premarket approval by the FDA. Included on the FDA Web site are the following articles: "FDA Alerts Consumers About Adverse Events Associated with 'Permanent Makeup'" and "Temporary Tattoos and Henna/Mehndi."

Health Canada

Communications, Marketing and Consultation Directorate
Ottawa, ON
  K1A 0K9
(613) 957-2983 • fax: (613) 952-7747
e-mail: info@hc-sc.gc.ca
Web site: www.hc-sc.gc.ca

Health Canada is the federal department responsible for helping Canadians maintain and improve their health. Its Web site includes many articles on the health risks of contracting infections or hepatitis as a result of tattoos or body piercing. Its publications include the following articles: "Tattooing and Piercing," and "Infection Prevention and Control Practices for Personal Services: Tattooing, Ear/Body Piercing, and Electrolysis."

Institute for Ethics and Emerging Technologies (IEET)

Williams 229B, Trinity College 300 Summit St.
Hartford, CT   06106
e-mail: director@ieet.org
Web site: http://ieet.org

IEET is an international organization that promotes a responsible and constructive approach to emerging human enhancement technologies. The organization's supporters defend individuals' rights to use human enhancement technologies—which include body modifications such as transdermal implants—while taking seriously the need to regulate their safety and social consequences. IEET's Web site includes a library of articles on tattoos, body piercings, and other forms of body modification. It publishes, along with other titles, the periodical *Journal of Evolution & Technology*.

National Institute of Environmental Health Sciences
P.O. Box 12233, Research Triangle Park, NC   27709
(919) 541-3345
Web site: www.niehs.nih.gov

With twenty-seven institutes and centers, the NIH is the primary federal agency for conducting and supporting medical research. As a component of the National Institutes of Health, NIEHS publishes on its Web site educational materials, including questions and answers about the health risks associated with body piercing and tattoos.

National Tattoo Association (NTA)
485 Business Park Lane, Allentown, PA   18109
e-mail: curt@nationaltatto.com
Web site: www.nationaltattooassociation.com

The NTA was founded to heighten awareness of tattooing as a contemporary art form and has developed into an organization that is dedicated to the advancement of safety, quality standards, and professionalism by tattoo artists. It offers advice on selecting a tattoo artist and studio. The NTA sponsors seminars for tattoo artists who want to improve their skills. Its publications include a bimonthly newsletter.

Paul Rogers Tattoo Research Center
2804 San Pablo Ave., Berkeley, CA   94702
(510) 548-5895
e-mail: tattoo@tattooarchive.com
Web site: www.tattooarchive.com

The primary goal of the Paul Rogers Research Center is to preserve and document tattoo history and to promote the history of tattooing through education and research. Its Web site includes articles on the history of tattoos in various cultures around the world and naval traditions, as well as famous tattooed people.

Professional Piercing Information Systems

P.O. Box 637, Cathedral City, CA   92235
(909) 553-4411 • fax: (760) 770-4599
Web site: www.propiercing.com

Professional Piercing Information Systems provides standardized education and training addressing health and safety concerns for the professional body piercer. It was the first piercing organization to include training that is compliant with Occupational Safety and Health Administration regulations. It offers courses for the experienced as well as the brand new piercer. Its Web site includes articles on health and safety issues affecting piercers.

Society of Permanent Cosmetic Professionals (SPCP)

69 North Broadway, Des Plaines, IL   60016
(847) 635-1330 • fax: (847) 635-1326
Web site: www.spcp.org

The SPCP is the largest professional association for the permanent cosmetics industry. It promotes safety by providing educational materials both to its members and to the public about permanent cosmetic procedures. It sponsors annual conventions and conferences and has a training certificate examination for permanent cosmetic technicians. In addition, it publishes a quarterly newsletter and includes articles on its Web site.

World Transhumanist Association (WTA)

P.O. Box 128, Willington, CT   06279
e-mail: secretary@transhumanism.org
Web site: www.transhumanism.org

The World Transhumanist Association is an international nonprofit membership organization which advocates the ethical use of technology to expand human capacities. It supports the development of and access to new technologies that enable people to enjoy body modification and cosmetic enhancement. Its Web site includes a library of articles about body modification.

Bibliography

Books

Kim Addonizio and Cheryl Dumesnil
Dorothy Parker's Elbow: Tattoos on Writers, Writers on Tattoos. New York: Warner Books, 2002.

Michael Atkinson
Tattooed: The Sociogenesis of a Body Art. Toronto: University of Toronto Press, 2003.

Margo DeMello
Encyclopedia of Body Adornment. Westport, CT: Greenwood Press, 2007.

Mindy Fenske
Tattoos in American Visual Culture. New York: Palgrave Macmillan, 2007.

Kathlyn Gay and Christine Whittington
Tattooing, Piercing, and Scarification. Brookfield, CT: Millbrook Press, 2002.

Terisa Green
Ink: The Not-Just-Skin-Deep Guide to Getting a Tattoo. New York: New American Library, 2005.

Eleonora Habnit
Permanent Makeup and Reconstructive Tattooing. Atglen, PA: Schiffer Books, 2003.

Gary Lee Heard
Body Art: The Human Canvas—Ink and Steel. Portland, OR: Collectors Press, 2003.

Karen L. Hudson
Chick Ink. Avon, MA: Adams Media, 2007.

Icon Health Publications   *Body Piercing: A Medical Dictionary, Bibliography, and Annotated Research Guide to Internet References*. San Diego: Icon Health Group, 2004.

Jean-Chris Miller   *The Body Art Book: A Complete, Illustrated Guide to Tattoos, Piercings, and Other Body Modifications*. New York: Berkeley Books, 2004.

Victoria Pitts-Taylor   *In the Flesh: The Cultural Politics of Body Modification*. New York: Palgrave Macmillan, 2003.

John Wyatt   *Under My Skin*. Atglen, PA: Schiffer Books, 2003.

Periodicals

Lisa A. Baker   "Regulating Matters of Appearance: Tattoos and Other Body Art," *FBI Law Enforcement Bulletin*, February 2007.

C. Mark Brinkley   "Think Before You Ink: Consider the 4 'Cs,'" *Army Times*, March 22, 2007.

Debra Darvik   "Service with a Smile," *Newsweek*, July 12, 2004.

David M. Deci   "The Medical Implications of Body Art," *Patient Care for the Nurse Practitioner*, April 1, 2005.

Roberto Gazzeri and Sandro Mercuri   "Atypical Trigeminal Neuralgia Associated with Tongue Piercing," *Journal of the American Medical Association*, October 18, 2006.

Beth Howard — "Piercing Potentials," *National Jeweler*, January 1, 2004.

Mary Kosut — "An Ironic Fad," *Journal of Popular Culture*, December 2006.

Sandra K. Leman and Mary Plattner — "When Beautification of the Body Turns Ugly," *Clinical Advisor*, February 2007.

Andrew Marshall — "Time to Rethink the Ink? New Clinic Erases Tattoos," *Deseret News*, June 7, 2007.

Tom McGhee — "Workers, Companies Spar Over Tattoos, Piercings," *Denver Post*, August 14, 2005.

Donna I. Meltzer — "Complications of Body Piercing," *American Family Physician*, November 15, 2005.

Men's Health — "Body of Evidence," April 2003.

Anna Mulrine — "The Thrill Is Gone," *U.S. News & World Report*, November 6, 2005.

Antonya Nelson — "Inimitable Ink," *Texas Monthly*, June 2007.

Jan Norman — "A Piercing Question in the Workplace," *Orange Country Register*, June 20, 2005.

Lucille M. Ponte and Jennifer L. Gillan — "Gender Performance Over Job Performance: Body Art Work Rules and the Continuing Subordination of the Feminine," *Duke Journal of Gender Law & Policy*, January 2007.

Rick Reilly   "Ink-Stained Wretch," *Sports Illustrated*, May 9, 2005.

Teen Vogue   "Hole Truth," April 2006.

Laurel A. Van Buskirk   "New Developments on Tattoos and Body Piercing in the Workplace," *New Hampshire Business Review*, December 2005.

Pippa Wysong   "Modified: Are Piercings and Tattoos Safe?" *Current Health 2*, March 2006.

Katie Zezima   "Yes, the Military Needs Bodies. But Hold the Bodywork," *New York Times*, December 3, 2005.

Internet Sources

Joseph Farah   "Discriminate Against Tattoos, Piercings at Your Own Risk," October 20, 2006. www.WorldNetDaily.com.

Erik Hartwell   "The Body as a Canvas," March 24, 2007. www.Ezinearticles.com.

How Stuff Works   "How Tattoo Removal Works." www.howstuffworks.com.

Karen Hudson   "Piercing Gun vs the Needle." tattoo.about.com/cs/psafety/a/piercing_guns.htm.

Marisa Kakoulas   "Employment Discrimination: Be Careful What You Sue For," April 5, 2004. www.BMEZine.com.

Joy Marie Sever   "A Third of Americans with Tattoos
                         Say They Make Them Feel More
                         Sexy," October 8, 2003.
                         www.HarrisInteractive.com.

TeensHealth   "Body Piercing." www.kidshealth.org.

Index